Learning
LIBRARY
Math

grade 2

The basic skills your 2nd grader needs!

- **Addition & Subtraction**
- **Time & Money**
- **Fractions**
- **Measurement**

- **Geometry**
- **Graphing**
- **Probability**
- **Problem Solving**

- **Patterns & Algebra**

Editor: Kathy Wolf
Contributing Writer: Cynthia Holcomb
Copy Editors: Tracy Johnson, Carol Rawleigh
Contributing Artist: Cathy Spangler Bruce
Typesetters: Lynette Dickerson, Mark Rainey
Cover Illustration and Design: Nick Greenwood

Table of Contents

©2002 by THE EDUCATION CENTER, INC.
All rights reserved.
ISBN# 1-56234-477-3

Manufactured in the United States
10 9 8 7 6 5 4 3 2 1

Table of Contents

Numbers and Operations

Numbers and operations play a major role in your child's second-grade math instruction. This year, your child will become adept at solving addition problems with sums to 18 and subtraction with differences through 18. Memorizing these related facts or *fact families* is essential to success.

Second graders begin to take mental short cuts in computation such as adding doubles, adding numbers in a column to make 10, and using addition to check subtraction. Your second grader will decide whether to add or subtract to solve a word problem and determine if the problem contains extra information that won't be used in finding the solution.

Your child will be able to identify the *place value* of each numeral in a number. In our number system, the place of each digit determines how much it is worth (for example, 365 = three hundreds, six tens, and five ones). Writing a number this way is called *expanded notation*. Your child will be able to count, read, and write numbers to 1,000.

An important concept for your child to master this year is *regrouping* tens when adding or subtracting. (We used to call this *carrying* the tens or *borrowing* from the tens.) Regrouping tens across zeros (for example, 500–365) is even more difficult to master and takes repeated practice.

Many second graders are ready to learn the multiplication facts to 5. Multiplication is introduced as repeated addition of sets. Some children are eager to learn their facts to 10. Your child's teacher may also introduce the concept of division as equal sharing of a whole or dividing up a set of things into equal groups.

In summary, this year your second grader will learn to
- add and subtract to 18
- identify the place value of numbers to 1,000
- compare numbers up to 1,000 using the symbols <, >, and =
- solve two- and three-digit problems with regrouping
- round numbers to the nearest 10
- decide to add or subtract to solve word problems
- count by 2s, 3s, and 5s
- multiply by repeated adding
- divide by creating equal groups

Key Math Skills for Grade 2
Numbers and Operations

- Counting, reading, and writing whole numbers to 1,000

- Addition and subtraction to 18

- Addition and subtraction word problems: choosing the correct operation to solve a problem, identifying unnecessary information

- Subtraction: Using addition to check subtraction

- Number order: ones, tens, and hundreds

- Number order: counting by 2s, 3s, and 5s

- Place value: comparing numbers up to 1,000 using <, >, =

- Place value: rounding to the nearest ten

- Place value: expanded notation to 1,000 (for example, 362 = 3 hundreds + 6 tens + 2 ones)

- Addition: two-digit and three-digit with regrouping

- Subtraction: two-digit and three-digit with regrouping

- Addition and subtraction across zeros

- Multiplication: understanding the concept of repeated adding of groups of equal size

- Multiplication: facts to 5

- Multiplication: facts to 9

- Division: understanding the concept of equal sharing

Name _____

Hot Dog!

Solve the facts on the hot dogs.
Color **red** ketchup on the hot dogs with even sums.
Color **yellow** mustard on the hot dogs with odd sums.

9 + 2 =   5 + 9 =   3 + 8 =   7 + 4 =

6 + 9 =   7 + 2 =   7 + 5 =   6 + 6 =

9 + 7 =   9 + 4 =   2 + 6 =   7 + 8 =

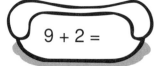

5 + 8 =   8 + 2 =   6 + 8 =

6 + 7 =   8 + 4 =   9 + 9 =

9 + 3 =   8 + 8 =

The tall man likes mustard.
The strong man likes ketchup.

The _____ man has
more hot dogs to eat.

At Home: With your child, talk about foods you might buy at a carnival or state fair. Help your child make a list of favorite fun foods. Then take turns creating addition problems for each other to solve, as you "eat your way" through the midway. (Example: What would you get if you ate nine snow cones and then three more? Answer: 12 snow cones and a tummy ache!)

Name _____

Tasty Treasure

In each treasure chest:
Solve each fact.
Cross out the matching sum on the lid.
Write the extra sum in the box.
Then write an addition fact that equals
  the sum.

A. 13 11 12

$7 + 5 =$ _____

$8 + 3 =$ _____

$=$ ⬜

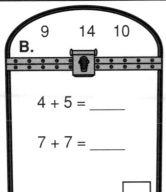

B. 9 14 10

$4 + 5 =$ _____

$7 + 7 =$ _____

$=$ ⬜

C. 7 8 11

$6 + 2 =$ _____

$2 + 9 =$ _____

$=$ ⬜

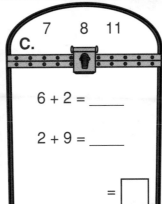

D. 14 15 13

$5 + 8 =$ _____

$9 + 5 =$ _____

$=$ ⬜

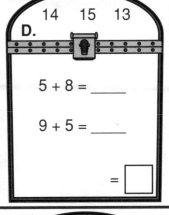

E. 9 8 11

$3 + 6 =$ _____

$5 + 3 =$ _____

$=$ ⬜

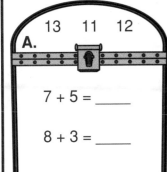

F. 12 14 15

$9 + 6 =$ _____

$4 + 8 =$ _____

$=$ ⬜

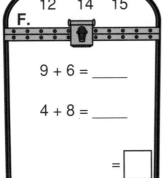

G. 10 11 12

$2 + 8 =$ _____

$7 + 4 =$ _____

$=$ ⬜

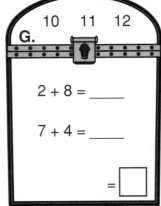

H. 15 12 16

$3 + 9 =$ _____

$8 + 7 =$ _____

$=$ ⬜

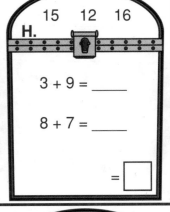

I. 10 9 11

$5 + 6 =$ _____

$6 + 4 =$ _____

$=$ ⬜

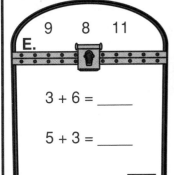

J. 17 16 18

$9 + 9 =$ _____

$8 + 8 =$ _____

$=$ ⬜

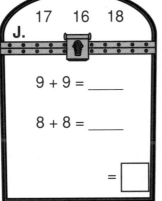

K. 7 9 8

$2 + 7 =$ _____

$3 + 4 =$ _____

$=$ ⬜

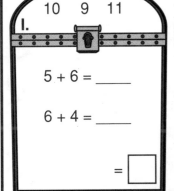

L. 6 9 12

$1 + 8 =$ _____

$6 + 6 =$ _____

$=$ ⬜

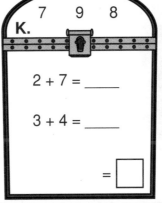

Name _____

A Space Race

Meet the Martians!
Solve each fact.

8 + 2 = _____   3 + 5 = _____

6 + 5 = _____   5 + 9 = _____

5 + 7 = _____

8 + 9 = _____

6 + 6 = _____   4 + 9 = _____

5 + 8 = _____   9 + 7 = _____

7 + 7 = _____   8 + 6 = _____

7 + 8 = _____

6 + 7 = _____

9 + 9 = _____   9 + 6 = _____

6 + 9 = _____   8 + 7 = _____

9 + 8 = _____   6 + 4 = _____

9 + 5 = _____

8 + 8 = _____

5 + 5 = _____   10 + 7 = _____

9 + 2 = _____   7 + 4 = _____

6 + 3 = _____

8 + 5 = _____   10 + 6 = _____

7 + 9 = _____

4 + 8 = _____   6 + 8 = _____

Look at the answers in each spaceship's smoke.
The Martian with the highest single answer is the winner.
Draw a blue ribbon on the winning spaceship.

Gliding Through the Galaxy

Solve the problems.
Cross out the answers on the planets and stars.

1.
```
  5
  6
+ 9
```

2.
```
  7
  8
+ 2
```

3.
```
  6
  6
+ 2
```

4.
```
  3
  6
+ 7
```

5.
```
  6
  9
+ 9
```

6.
```
  8
  1
+ 9
```

7.
```
  7
  9
+ 3
```

8.
```
  2
  3
+ 8
```

9.
```
  5
  6
+ 3
```

10.
```
  7
  3
+ 7
```

11.
```
  2
  6
+ 5
```

12.
```
  3
  7
+ 2
```

13.
```
  6
  5
+ 4
```

14.
```
  6
  7
+ 3
```

15.
```
  4
  7
+ 5
```

16.
```
  9
  1
+ 2
```

17.
```
  5
  4
+ 4
```

18.
```
  6
  5
+ 6
```

19.
```
  2
  9
+ 3
```

20.
```
  7
  9
+ 4
```

21.
```
  6
  3
+ 5
```

Planets and stars: 14, 14, 24, 19, 16, 20, 17, 15, 12, 14, 13, 16, 12, 13, 20, 17, 16, 18, 17, 13, 14

Try This: If each Martian has three eyes, how many eyes will three Martians have? Draw a picture that shows your answer.

Grinning Giraffes

Solve the facts.

5	2	7	8	1
+ 8	+ 9	+ 7	+ 6	+ 4

7 + 5 = _____   4 + 4 = _____   9 + 4 = _____

5 + 6 = _____   8 + 8 = _____   5 + 9 = _____

8 + 9 = _____   3 + 8 = _____   7 + 9 = _____

6 + 7 = _____   9 + 9 = _____   6 + 3 = _____

2 + 5 = _____   4 + 7 = _____   8 + 3 = _____

Try This:
Draw an orange circle around each sum that is greater than 10. You should have 18 circles.

7	4	8	9	3
+ 8	+ 5	+ 2	+ 6	+ 7

Where Is That Lion?

Solve the facts.

18 − 9 = _____   13 − 6 = _____   12 − 9 = _____   14 − 6 = _____

                     14 − 9 = _____   13 − 5 = _____   11 − 4 = _____

16	15	10	16	14	11
− 8	− 9	− 6	− 9	− 5	− 7

17	11	16	12	13
− 8	− 2	− 7	− 7	− 8

13 − 4 = _____   15 − 7 = _____

12 − 5 = _____   13 − 7 = _____

Try This:
If you have six facts that equal nine, color the lion's nose pink.

Hide-and-Seek

Solve each fact.
Cross out a matching answer on the bush.

12	18	9	8	11	3
− 8	− 9	+ 5	+ 8	− 6	+ 9

7	8	17	15	9	15	14
+ 6	+ 7	− 9	− 8	+ 7	− 6	− 8

13	6	9
− 6	+ 5	+ 8

7
13   16
5   12
15   17   9
11   4
6   16   8
14   9   7

Some Monkey Business

Solve the facts.

3	6	15	6	12	8	13
+ 8	+ 8	− 7	+ 9	− 6	+ 9	− 5

8	14	9	8	13	16
+ 5	− 7	+ 9	+ 4	− 8	− 7

9	12	16	13	7
+ 7	− 3	− 8	− 9	+ 7

MONKEYS

Name _____

Ferris Wheel Figures

Solve the problems.
Write the answers.

$$\begin{array}{r}12\\+\ 2\\\hline\end{array}$$

$$\begin{array}{r}73\\+\ 4\\\hline\end{array}$$

$$\begin{array}{r}42\\+\ 3\\\hline\end{array}$$

$$\begin{array}{r}62\\+\ 5\\\hline\end{array}$$

$$\begin{array}{r}36\\+\ 3\\\hline\end{array}$$

$$\begin{array}{r}54\\+\ 1\\\hline\end{array}$$

$$\begin{array}{r}24\\+\ 2\\\hline\end{array}$$

$$\begin{array}{r}33\\+\ 3\\\hline\end{array}$$

$$\begin{array}{r}16\\+\ 2\\\hline\end{array}$$

$$\begin{array}{r}18\\+\ 1\\\hline\end{array}$$

$$\begin{array}{r}53\\+\ 4\\\hline\end{array}$$

$$\begin{array}{r}23\\+\ 6\\\hline\end{array}$$

$$\begin{array}{r}47\\+\ 2\\\hline\end{array}$$

$$\begin{array}{r}11\\+\ 5\\\hline\end{array}$$

Name _____

Bumper Buddies

Solve each problem.
Color a ◯ on the car below with the matching answer.

23 + 4	32 + 3	72 + 7	81 + 1	61 + 3
62 + 2	42 + 4	22 + 5	43 + 3	51 + 7
53 + 5	74 + 5	63 + 1	54 + 4	70 + 9
73 + 6	34 + 1	52 + 6	71 + 8	41 + 5

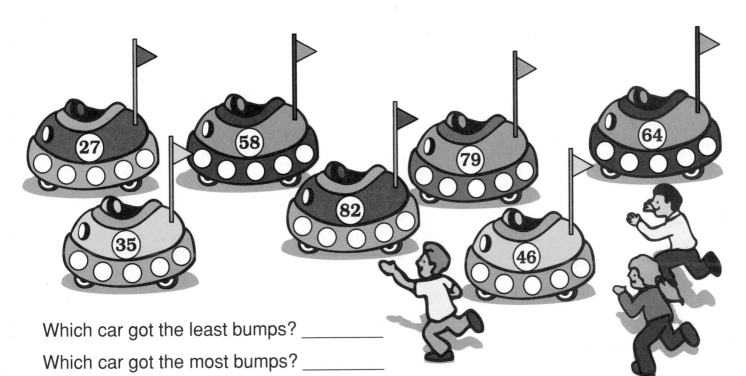

Which car got the least bumps? _____

Which car got the most bumps? _____

Carousel Ride

Solve each problem.

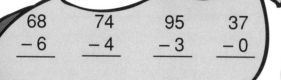

$$\begin{array}{r} 68 \\ -6 \\ \hline \end{array} \quad \begin{array}{r} 74 \\ -4 \\ \hline \end{array} \quad \begin{array}{r} 95 \\ -3 \\ \hline \end{array} \quad \begin{array}{r} 37 \\ -0 \\ \hline \end{array}$$

$$\begin{array}{r} 26 \\ -2 \\ \hline \end{array} \quad \begin{array}{r} 38 \\ -5 \\ \hline \end{array} \quad \begin{array}{r} 17 \\ -1 \\ \hline \end{array} \quad \begin{array}{r} 59 \\ -5 \\ \hline \end{array}$$

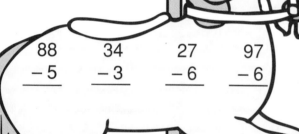

$$\begin{array}{r} 88 \\ -5 \\ \hline \end{array} \quad \begin{array}{r} 34 \\ -3 \\ \hline \end{array} \quad \begin{array}{r} 27 \\ -6 \\ \hline \end{array} \quad \begin{array}{r} 97 \\ -6 \\ \hline \end{array}$$

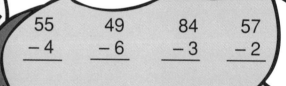

$$\begin{array}{r} 55 \\ -4 \\ \hline \end{array} \quad \begin{array}{r} 49 \\ -6 \\ \hline \end{array} \quad \begin{array}{r} 84 \\ -3 \\ \hline \end{array} \quad \begin{array}{r} 57 \\ -2 \\ \hline \end{array}$$

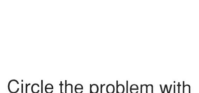
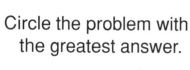

Circle the problem with
the greatest answer.

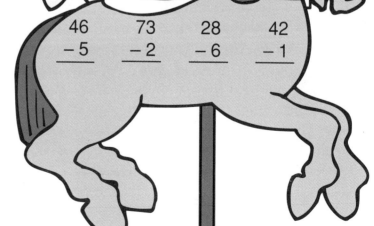

$$\begin{array}{r} 46 \\ -5 \\ \hline \end{array} \quad \begin{array}{r} 73 \\ -2 \\ \hline \end{array} \quad \begin{array}{r} 28 \\ -6 \\ \hline \end{array} \quad \begin{array}{r} 42 \\ -1 \\ \hline \end{array}$$

Name _____

Solve each problem.
Show your work on
the boxcar.

Calculation Station

← To Trains

1. A train has 13 boxcars.
   2 more are added.
   How many in all?

2. A train has 27 flatcars.
   2 are taken away.
   How many are left?

3. A train has 16 tank cars.
   3 more are added.
   How many in all?

4. A train has 39 passengers.
   4 get off.
   How many are left?

5. A train travels 41 miles.
   It travels 8 more miles.
   How many in all?

6. A rack car carries 12 cars.
   2 cars are taken off.
   How many are left?

7. A train has 26 boxcars.
   It has 5 flatcars.
   How many more boxcars?

8. A train has 41 cars.
   2 flatcars are added.
   3 tank cars are added.
   How many in all?

9. There are 17 cars in a train.
   Some are blue and some
     are yellow.
   5 of the cars are blue.
   How many are yellow?

10. There are 29 cars in a train.
    5 hopper cars are taken off.
    4 boxcars are taken off.
    How many are left?

Adding With Ten Frames

Use the picture to answer each question.
Then solve the problem.

A. How many tens? _____
How many ones? _____

$$\begin{array}{r} 12 \\ + 11 \\ \hline \end{array}$$

B. How many tens? _____
How many ones? _____

$$\begin{array}{r} 11 \\ + 7 \\ \hline \end{array}$$

C. How many tens? _____
How many ones? _____

$$\begin{array}{r} 13 \\ + 16 \\ \hline \end{array}$$

D. How many tens? _____
How many ones? _____

$$\begin{array}{r} 12 \\ + 4 \\ \hline \end{array}$$

E. How many tens? _____
How many ones? _____

$$\begin{array}{r} 14 \\ + 14 \\ \hline \end{array}$$

F. How many tens? _____
How many ones? _____

$$\begin{array}{r} 16 \\ + 12 \\ \hline \end{array}$$

G. How many tens? _____
How many ones? _____

$$\begin{array}{r} 15 \\ + 13 \\ \hline \end{array}$$

H. How many tens? _____
How many ones? _____

$$\begin{array}{r} 11 \\ + 8 \\ \hline \end{array}$$

Try This: Count the number of lamps in your house. Then count the number of lightbulbs. Make ten frames to show the number of each. Then add to find the total of both.

Name_____

Going Buggy!

Write the number that comes just **after**.

 1. 7

 2. 14

 3. 18

 4. 20

 5. 29

 6. 33

 7. 39

 8. 46

 9. 48

Write the number that comes just **before**.

10. 19

11. 8

12. 13

13. 50

14. 10

15. 27

16. 24

17. 30

18. 41

Write the number that comes **in between**.

 19. 17 ___ 19

 20. 30 ___ 32

 21. 24 ___ 26

 22. 39 ___ 41

 23. 10 ___ 12

 24. 46 ___ 48

At Home: Have your child count by 2s with you. You say the odd numbers while your child says the even numbers.

Name _____

How Sweet It Is!

Circle the larger number in each pair.
Color the jelly bean if the larger number is odd.

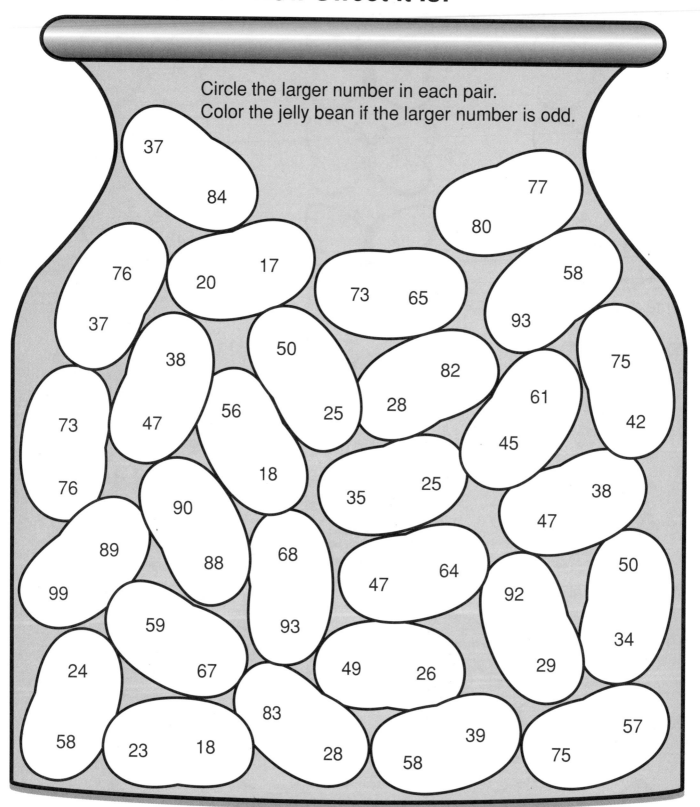

At Home: Secretly, place a number of jelly beans or wrapped candies in a glass jar. Ask each member of the family to guess the number and to write his or her estimate on a piece of paper. Then, have your child count the candies and compare to each estimated answer. Who guessed more? Who guessed less? Whose guess was closest? Was the number even or odd? Share the estimates and the treats.

Number order
Ones, tens, and hundreds

Shell Shocked!

Write > or < to make each
sentence true.

113 ___ 98

624 ___ 900

507 ___ 298

803 ___ 309

412 ___ 406

360 ___ 485

413 ___ 802

764 ___ 317

128 ___ 218

392 ___ 615

925 ___ 952

413 ___ 598

754 ___ 275

927 ___ 940

728 ___ 635

461 ___ 527

649 ___ 714

487 ___ 198

258 ___ 303

At Home: Which number is larger: the last 3 digits of your phone number or the last three digits of your zip code?

19

Name_____

"Whooooo's" Stargazing?

Answer the problems in order.
Write your answers on the lines.
Use each number only one time.
When you use a number,
  color its star yellow.

Hooty's
Home

1. Which number is greatest? _____	2. Which number is least? _____	3. Which number is greater than 48 and less than 61? _____
4. Which two numbers are less than 90 and greater than 62? _____ _____	5. Complete each number sentence. _____ < 32 _____ > 45	6. Two numbers remain. Use them to complete this sentence. _____ > _____
7. Write a number in the blank star that is less than the other numbers.	8. Use the remaining number to complete this math sentence. Draw a symbol in the circle. _____ ◯ 78	**Try This:** Write a number sentence that compares the ages of your mom and dad.

Stars: 26, 34, 40, 71, 59, 17, 95, 83, 62

Name _____

A Mission From Mars

Help the Martian solve the problems.

35 + 11	41 + 17	17 + 22

32 + 16	39 + 10	13 + 12	55 + 43	30 + 32

49 + 30	25 + 51	23 + 36	15 + 14	32 + 57

11 + 84	66 + 21	73 + 26	64 + 33	57 + 31

Try This: Circle each odd answer.

Name _____

Rocket Regrouping

When the sum in the ones place is more than 9, regroup to the tens place.

Example:

tens	ones
☐ 1	5
+ 1	7

5 + 7 = 12. Write the 2 in the ones place.
Regroup the ten to the tens place.

Like this:

tens	ones
1 1	5
+ 1	7
3	2

Now add these numbers.

1.

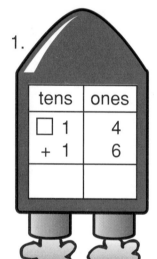

tens	ones
☐ 1	4
+ 1	6

2.

tens	ones
☐ 2	7
+ 1	3

3.

tens	ones
☐ 2	8
+ 2	4

4.

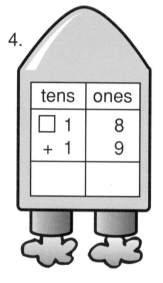

tens	ones
☐ 1	8
+ 1	9

5.

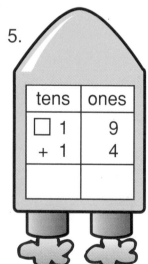

tens	ones
☐ 1	9
+ 1	4

6.

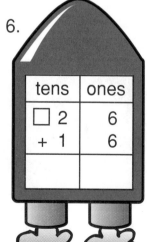

tens	ones
☐ 2	6
+ 1	6

7.

tens	ones
☐ 3	3
+	8

8.

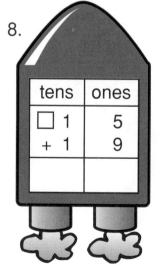

tens	ones
☐ 1	5
+ 1	9

Destination: Earth

Solve the problems.
Show your work.
Use the color code to color the
  spaceships.

Color Code

85 – 95 = blue

65 – 84 = green

50 – 64 = yellow

30 – 49 = red

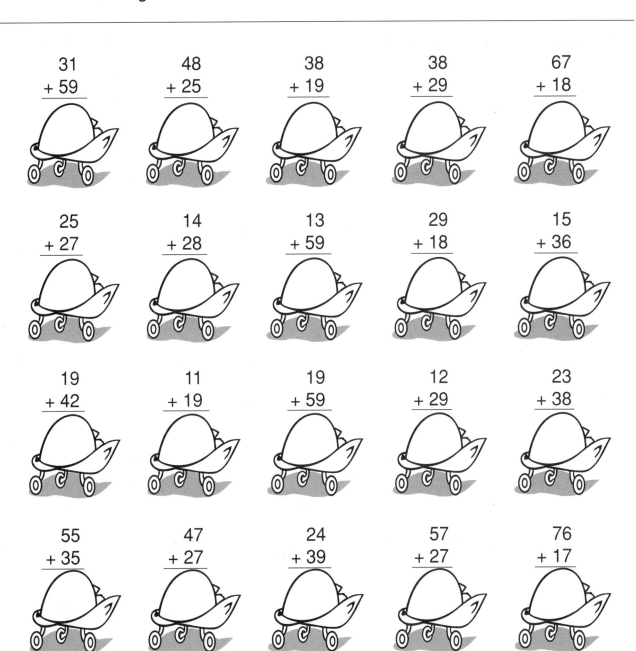

31 + 59	48 + 25	38 + 19	38 + 29	67 + 18
25 + 27	14 + 28	13 + 59	29 + 18	15 + 36
19 + 42	11 + 19	19 + 59	12 + 29	23 + 38
55 + 35	47 + 27	24 + 39	57 + 27	76 + 17

A Real "Mathful"

Solve the problems.
Show your work.

• 6   • 8   • 10
• 4   • 12
• 2
• 14
★ 0
• 48   • 16
• 46   • 18
• 44   • 20
• 42   • 22
• 24
• 40
• 38   • 26
• 36   • 34 • 30 • 28 • 32

$$45 + 27$$ $$64 + 16$$ $$23 + 28$$ $$39 + 46$$

$$51 + 39$$ $$46 + 26$$ $$15 + 78$$ $$48 + 27$$

$$17 + 79$$ $$58 + 16$$ $$44 + 18$$ $$53 + 27$$

$$64 + 27$$ $$78 + 19$$ $$36 + 55$$ $$21 + 49$$

$$16 + 79$$ $$57 + 36$$ $$26 + 17$$ $$33 + 29$$

Count by twos to connect the dots.

At Home: Save your cash register receipts from the grocery store. Cut the register tapes apart to create addition problems with two-digit numbers. Place the slips of paper in a zippered plastic sandwich bag. Have your child pull out one or two problems a day to practice.

Secret Sandwich

Solve the problems.
Match the letters to the numbered lines
  below to solve the riddle.

What is the
best-selling sandwich
at the Silly Sandwich Shop?

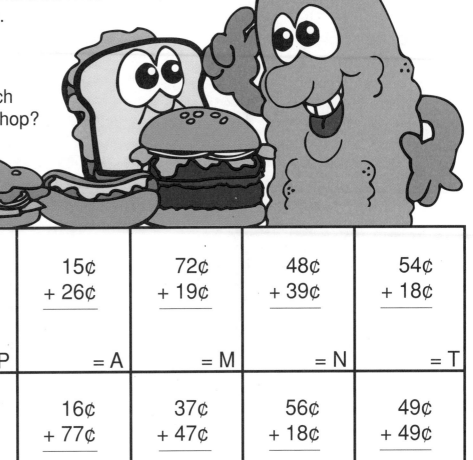

36¢ + 45¢ = D	57¢ + 28¢ = P	15¢ + 26¢ = A	72¢ + 19¢ = M	48¢ + 39¢ = N	54¢ + 18¢ = T
54¢ + 38¢ = E	25¢ + 17¢ = R	16¢ + 77¢ = U	37¢ + 47¢ = B	56¢ + 18¢ = T	49¢ + 49¢ = U
39¢ + 11¢ = T	76¢ + 14¢ = U	51¢ + 19¢ = A	22¢ + 29¢ = T	13¢ + 18¢ = S	31¢ + 29¢ = E

___ ___ ___ ___ ___ ___   ___ ___ ___ ___ ___ ___ ___ and
85¢ 60¢ 70¢ 87¢ 90¢ 72¢   84¢ 93¢ 51¢ 74¢ 92¢ 42¢

___ ___ ___ ___ ___ ___ ___
91¢ 98¢ 31¢ 50¢ 41¢ 42¢ 81¢

Name_____

Riding to the Top!

Solve the problems.
Show your work.

Why did the "unhoppy" bunny decide to go snow skiing?

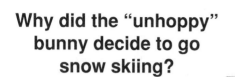

LOST
HAT
PASS

16 + 15 = E	26 + 27 = H
17 + 24 = E	49 + 23 = N	57 + 37 = S
26 + 19 = L	36 + 54 = A	19 + 45 = B

38 + 23 = E	55 + 15 = I	37 + 38 = E	37 + 45 = D	49 + 19 = U	45 + 46 = T
68 + 15 = A	48 + 38 = E	38 + 19 = D	17 + 59 = F	57 + 23 = C	29 + 48 = E

To solve the riddle, match the letters to the numbered lines below.

‾64‾ ‾41‾ ‾80‾ ‾83‾ ‾68‾ ‾94‾ ‾86‾   ‾53‾ ‾75‾

‾72‾ ‾61‾ ‾31‾ ‾57‾ ‾77‾ ‾82‾   ‾90‾   ‾45‾ ‾70‾ ‾76‾ ‾91‾!

Name_____

Full Speed Ahead!

Solve each subtraction problem.
Check your work by adding.
The first one is done for you!

Example:

a.
$$\begin{array}{r} 7\ 14 \\ \cancel{84} \\ -25 \\ \hline 59 \end{array} \quad \begin{array}{r} 1 \\ 59 \\ +25 \\ \hline 84 \end{array}$$

b.
$$\begin{array}{r} 89 \\ -29 \\ \hline \end{array} + \underline{}$$

c.
$$\begin{array}{r} 72 \\ -34 \\ \hline \end{array} + \underline{}$$

d.
$$\begin{array}{r} 53 \\ -17 \\ \hline \end{array} + \underline{}$$

e.
$$\begin{array}{r} 79 \\ -54 \\ \hline \end{array} + \underline{}$$

f.
$$\begin{array}{r} 63 \\ -29 \\ \hline \end{array} + \underline{}$$

g.
$$\begin{array}{r} 76 \\ -32 \\ \hline \end{array} + \underline{}$$

h.
$$\begin{array}{r} 86 \\ -47 \\ \hline \end{array} + \underline{}$$

i.
$$\begin{array}{r} 54 \\ -26 \\ \hline \end{array} + \underline{}$$

j.
$$\begin{array}{r} 62 \\ -19 \\ \hline \end{array} + \underline{}$$

k.
$$\begin{array}{r} 96 \\ -55 \\ \hline \end{array} + \underline{}$$

l.
$$\begin{array}{r} 26 \\ -18 \\ \hline \end{array} + \underline{}$$

n.
$$\begin{array}{r} 85 \\ -43 \\ \hline \end{array} + \underline{}$$

m.
$$\begin{array}{r} 43 \\ -28 \\ \hline \end{array} + \underline{}$$

o.
$$\begin{array}{r} 85 \\ -64 \\ \hline \end{array} + \underline{}$$

p.
$$\begin{array}{r} 79 \\ -36 \\ \hline \end{array} + \underline{}$$

At Home: Purchase a large bag of stick pretzels to provide practice with subtraction. Give your child ten empty, zippered plastic bags. Have him count and place ten pretzels in each bag. Put aside a bowl of twenty single pretzels for regrouping purposes. Have your child choose a problem on the page and make each number by gathering bags of tens and ones. To add, have him add the ones and trade in ten pretzels for a bag of ten. No snacking 'till the answer is correct!

Punny Pancakes

Read the riddle below.
Add or subtract. Show your work.

Riddle: What is a pancake's favorite fairy tale?

1. 48 + 23 L	2. 50 − 25 A	3. 71 − 35 A	4. 19 + 11 S
5. 97 − 18 D	6. 27 + 18 G	7. 80 − 52 L	8. 91 − 73 R
9. 57 − 28 H	10. 31 + 29 E	11. 63 − 24 E	12. 38 + 16 N
13. 39 + 55 I	14. 19 + 31 N	15. 59 + 11 D	16. 62 − 46 D

Write the letter that matches each answer to discover the answer to the riddle.

Answer:

                                                    "   "

__ __ __ __ __ __   __ __ __   __ __ __ __ __ __ __
29 36 54 30 39 71   25 50 16   45 18 94 79 70 28 60

Penguin Party

Read each problem.
Cross out the number you don't need to answer the question.
Then solve the problem.

1. Petey Penguin is planning a party.
   He bought 12 red balloons, 7 green balloons, and 20 party hats.
   How many balloons did he buy in all?

2. Peggy is helping Petey with the food.
   She made 2 cakes and 14 jelly sandwiches. She ate 3 of the sandwiches.
   How many sandwiches does she have left?

3. Petey invited 20 penguins to the party.
   Six penguins will be out of town and 2 will be coming in a new car.
   How many of the penguins invited will be at the party?

4. Petey wants to have prizes for the party games.
   He bought 9 blue ribbons, 8 gold medals, and 2 boxes to put them in.
   How many prizes did he buy altogether?

5. Peggy's camera has 18 pictures left on the film.
   Last year she took 10 pictures at the party. She will take 12 pictures tonight.
   How many pictures will she have left?

6. Pam is going to sing at the party.
   She has learned 13 fast songs, 5 slow songs, and 11 new dance steps.
   How many songs has she learned?

7. Pam helped Petey set up for the party.
   They moved 3 tables, 6 benches, and 8 chairs.
   How many things are there for them to sit on?

8. Peggy and Pam will give each guest something to wear.
   There are 9 blue hats, 6 fancy headbands, and 7 yellow hats.
   How many hats are there?

Great Gumballs!

Read each word problem.
Solve each problem on another piece of paper.
Write the answer in the blank. Then color the correct gumball.

1. Susan bought 48 pieces of gum on Thursday. By Saturday she had chewed 9 pieces. How many pieces of gum does Susan have left?

   _____

2. Kiesha bought 3 packs of peppermint gum. Each pack cost 25¢. How much money did Kiesha spend? _____

3. Lin has 12 gumballs. Meg has 19. How many gumballs do Lin and Meg have altogether?

   _____

4. Eric bought 2 packs of gum at the store. Each pack of gum has 14 sticks. How many sticks in all? _____

5. Molly had 50 gumballs. She gave 23 of them to Sam. How many gumballs does Molly have left? _____

6. Raj has 80¢ to spend on gum. How many 10¢ gumballs can Raj buy at the candy store?

   _____

7. Tim has 18 sticks of gum, Ed has 20 sticks of gum, and Kevin has 14 sticks of gum. How many sticks of gum do Tim, Ed, and Kevin have altogether? _____

8. Jeff had 75¢. He bought a pack of gum for 25¢. How much change will Jeff get back? _____

9. Josh bought 33 gumballs at the store. He gave his sister 9 gumballs. How many gumballs does Josh have left? _____

10. Julio had 95¢ to spend at the market. He bought a pack of mint gum for 49¢. How much money does Julio have left? _____

Name_____

Mmmm! Hot Chocolate!

Read each problem carefully.
Solve each one.
Write your answer on the line.

1. Kandi put 10 marshmallows in her hot chocolate. Randy put 6 marsh-mallows in his hot chocolate. 2 of Kandi's marshmallows melted. How many marshmallows were left in Kandi's hot chocolate?

   _____

2. Randy drank 4 mugs of hot chocolate. Kandi drank 2 mugs of hot chocolate. There are 2 mugs of hot chocolate left. How many mugs of hot chocolate did Randy and Kandi drink together?

   _____

3. Kandi made 5 mugs of instant hot chocolate. Randy made 4 mugs of hot chocolate with milk. 3 mugs were not drunk. How many more mugs of hot chocolate did Kandi make than Randy?

   _____

4. Randy and Kandi had a party on February 10. Randy served 9 mugs of hot chocolate. Kandi served 2 mugs of hot chocolate. How many more mugs of hot chocolate did Randy serve than Kandi?

   _____

5. Randy put whipped cream on 8 mugs of hot chocolate. He left 5 mugs plain. 3 mugs with whipped cream were drunk. How many mugs with whipped cream were left?

   _____

6. Kandi drank 2 mugs of hot chocolate in 2 weeks. Randy drank 6 mugs of hot chocolate in 4 weeks. How many mugs of hot chocolate did Kandi and Randy drink altogether?

   _____

7. Kandi's family drank 3 mugs of hot chocolate for breakfast. Randy's family drank 2 mugs of hot chocolate at lunch. Kandi's family drank 4 mugs of hot chocolate after dinner. How many mugs of hot chocolate did Kandi's family drink altogether?

   _____

8. Randy's mother made 6 mugs of hot chocolate for an afternoon snack. Kandi drank 2 mugs of hot chocolate. Randy drank 1 mug of hot chocolate. How many mugs of hot chocolate did Kandi and Randy drink altogether?

   _____

At Home: Provide a bag of mini-marshmallows to use as manipulative counters to act out the problems.

Name _____

It's Bake Sale Time!

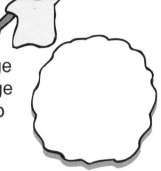

Read each problem carefully.
Solve each problem on the cookie.
Show your work.

1. Kandi made 64 small chocolate chip cookies and 8 large peanut butter bars for the bake sale. Cyndi made 9 large chocolate chip cookies. How many more chocolate chip cookies did Kandi make than Cyndi?

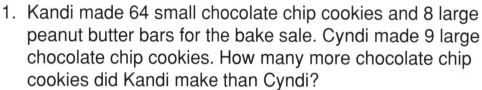

2. Randy brought 2 plates of chocolate fudge cookies. One plate had 8 cookies on it. The other had 36 cookies on it. Each cookie sold for 5¢. How many cookies did Randy bring in all?

3. Kandi sold 5 plain brownies for 10¢ each. She sold 25 chocolate drop cookies for 5¢ each. She also sold 27 frosted brownies for 15¢ each. How many brownies did Kandi sell altogether?

4. There was a total of 96 chocolate drop cookies on 3 plates. Randy sold 38 cookies. Kandi sold 9. How many chocolate drop cookies did Randy and Kandi sell altogether?

5. Kandi will need 8 cherries and 1 bag of chocolate chips to make choco-cherry cookies. A bag of chocolate chips has 72 chips in it. How many more chocolate chips than cherries does Kandi need?

6. Randy sold 8 pieces of fudge. Kandi sold 31. Their teacher sold 26. How many more pieces of fudge did Kandi sell than Randy?

Bake Sale
TODAY!

Name _____

A Chocolate Lover's Fantasy

Read each problem carefully.
Solve each one.
Show your work.

1. A pint of chocolate milk costs 13¢. A quart of chocolate milk costs 27¢. How much more does a quart of chocolate milk cost than a pint?

2. A chocolate chip cookie costs 22¢. A chocolate fudgie costs 16¢. How much more does a chocolate chip cookie cost than a chocolate fudgie?

3. Kandi has 38¢. Ice-cream bars cost 25¢ each. Kandi buys one bar. How much money does Kandi have left?

4. Randy has 46¢. He buys a chocolate drop for 14¢. How much money does Randy have left?

5. The candy store has chocolate bars for 18¢ each. They also have chocolate nut bars for 23¢ each. If Randy buys one of each, how much money does he need?

6. Kandi bought a small chocolate ice-cream cone for 15¢. Randy bought a large ice-cream cone for 32¢. How much did the ice-cream cones cost altogether?

7. A piece of chocolate fudge cake costs 35¢. A piece of German chocolate cake costs 28¢. How much more does a slice of chocolate fudge cake cost than a slice of German chocolate cake?

8. Kandi bought a slice of chocolate cream pie for Randy for 24¢. She bought a slice of mud pie for herself for 19¢. How much did Kandi spend altogether?

Name _____

Feeding on the Facts

Solve each problem.
Cross out the matching answer in the fish.
Hint: There are three extra fish.

Example: 1.
$$\begin{array}{r} \overset{1}{1}45 \\ + 236 \\ \hline 381 \end{array}$$

2.
$$\begin{array}{r} 252 \\ + 471 \\ \hline \end{array}$$

3.
$$\begin{array}{r} 631 \\ + 229 \\ \hline \end{array}$$

4.
$$\begin{array}{r} 427 \\ + 392 \\ \hline \end{array}$$

5.
$$\begin{array}{r} 668 \\ + 123 \\ \hline \end{array}$$

6.
$$\begin{array}{r} 444 \\ + 261 \\ \hline \end{array}$$

7.
$$\begin{array}{r} 378 \\ + 312 \\ \hline \end{array}$$

8.
$$\begin{array}{r} 821 \\ + 129 \\ \hline \end{array}$$

9.
$$\begin{array}{r} 117 \\ + 336 \\ \hline \end{array}$$

10.
$$\begin{array}{r} 432 \\ + 193 \\ \hline \end{array}$$

11.
$$\begin{array}{r} 247 \\ + 118 \\ \hline \end{array}$$

12.
$$\begin{array}{r} 581 \\ + 297 \\ \hline \end{array}$$

13.
$$\begin{array}{r} 221 \\ + 696 \\ \hline \end{array}$$

14.
$$\begin{array}{r} 670 \\ + 159 \\ \hline \end{array}$$

15.
$$\begin{array}{r} 103 \\ + 118 \\ \hline \end{array}$$

Fish numbers: 453, 829, 860, 625, 705, 927, 365, 819, 221, 791, 690, 878, 222, 950, 917, 723, 381, 839

Get Ready for a Parade

Solve each problem.
Connect the answers in order from the least to the greatest to discover the parade
route.

137
+ 263

249
+ 176

308
+ 272

317
+ 197

268
+ 316

184
+ 257

299
+ 211

274
+ 327

361
+ 148

448
+ 183

286
+ 336

537
+ 277

481
+ 239

519
+ 234

536
+ 374

Meet the Count!

Count! Count! Count!
Count by twos, threes, or fives.
Write a numeral in each blank to
complete the pattern.

A. 10, ___, ___, ___, 30, ___, ___, ___, ___

B. 6, 9, ___, ___, ___, 21, ___, ___, ___

C. 8, ___, ___, ___, 16, ___, ___, ___, ___

D. 18, ___, ___, ___, 30, ___, ___, ___, ___

E. 45, ___, ___, ___, ___, 70, ___, ___, ___

F. 34, ___, ___, ___, 42, ___, ___, ___

G. 40, ___, ___, ___, ___, 50, ___, ___, ___

H. 30, ___, ___, ___, 42, ___, ___, ___, ___

If you counted by twos, draw a circle in front of the row.
If you counted by threes, draw a square in front of the row.
If you counted by fives, draw a triangle in front of the row.

Name _____

Count on This Crop!

Count by 2s, 3s, or 5s.
Write a numeral in each blank to complete the pattern.
Then color a fruit or vegetable to show the number
  pattern you used.

1.   10, 12, 14, _____, _____, _____, 22, _____, _____, _____

2.   3, 6, 9, _____, _____, 18, _____, _____, _____, _____

3.   35, 40, 45, _____, _____, _____, _____, 70, _____, _____

4.   21, 24, 27, _____, _____, _____, _____, _____, _____, 48

5.   55, 60, 65, _____, 75, _____, _____, _____, _____, _____

6.   72, 75, 78, _____, _____, _____, 90, _____, _____, _____

7.   36, 39, 42, _____, _____, _____, _____, 57, _____, _____

8.   64, 66, 68, _____, _____, _____, 76, _____, _____, _____

9.   15, 20, 25, _____, _____, _____, _____, _____, 55, _____

10.   48, 50, 52, _____, _____, _____, _____, 62, _____, _____

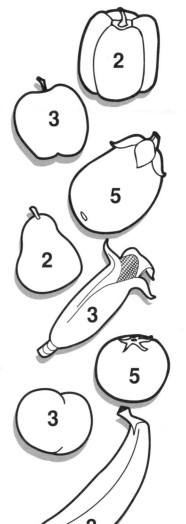

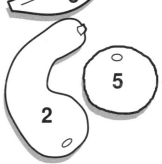

At Home: Make a collection of 100 objects such as pennies, dried
beans, or toothpicks. Count the objects aloud with your child. Then
help him make groups of ten and use the groups as you both count
by tens to 100. Repeat with groups of five and two.

Name _____

Pond Pals

Leaping Larry wants to visit Hopping Harry.
To complete his path, skip-count by 4s.
Write each number in order.

Name _____

Frolicking Froggies

Round the number on each lily pad
  to the nearest ten.
Follow the rounding rule.
Write each answer on the blank.

Rounding Rule
If the number in the ones place is
5 or more, round up—
less than 5, round down

A. 27

B. 73

C. 6

D. 52

E. 38

F. 64

G. 18

H. 43

I. 66

J. 94

K. 21

L. 77

M. 89

N. 31

O. 82

P. 59

Color each lily pad.
If you rounded up, color it green.
If you rounded down, color it yellow.

Name _____

Pumpkin Patch Math

Write each number in expanded notation.

146 — 100 + 40 + 6

272 — ___ + ___ + ___

568 — ___ + ___ + ___

421 — ___ + ___ + ___

739 — ___ + ___ + ___

396 — ___ + ___ + ___

940 — ___ + ___ + ___

118 — ___ + ___ + ___

677 — ___ + ___ + ___

843 — ___ + ___ + ___

459 — ___ + ___ + ___

Write each number in standard form.

200 + 80 + 4 — 284

400 + 30 + 4 — _____

900 + 20 + 9 — _____

700 + 70 + 3 — _____

100 + 60 + 2 — _____

800 + 10 + 5 — _____

300 + 60 + 2 — _____

500 + 50 + 3 — _____

400 + 90 + 1 — _____

700 + 30 + 8 — _____

600 + 40 + 7 — _____

Name _____

Pumpkin Pals

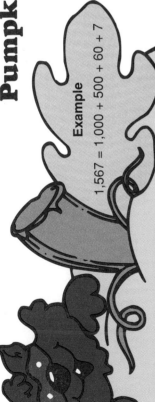

Example
1,567 = 1,000 + 500 + 60 + 7

Example
3,000 + 800 + 70 + 6 = 3,876

Write each number in expanded notation.

4,763 = _____ + _____ + _____ + _____

5,842 = _____ + _____ + _____ + _____

2,391 = _____ + _____ + _____ + _____

7,287 = _____ + _____ + _____ + _____

9,564 = _____ + _____ + _____ + _____

6,469 = _____ + _____ + _____ + _____

1,725 = _____ + _____ + _____ + _____

3,927 = _____ + _____ + _____ + _____

8,659 = _____ + _____ + _____ + _____

1,843 = _____ + _____ + _____ + _____

Write each number in standard form.

3,000 + 700 + 80 + 5 = _____

1,000 + 400 + 60 + 2 = _____

6,000 + 300 + 50 + 1 = _____

4,000 + 900 + 40 + 9 = _____

2,000 + 600 + 70 + 7 = _____

5,000 + 100 + 10 + 8 = _____

8,000 + 300 + 20 + 6 = _____

4,000 + 200 + 90 + 3 = _____

9,000 + 500 + 30 + 2 = _____

7,000 + 800 + 50 + 5 = _____

Name _____

Turkey Turnabout

Look at the numerals on each set of feathers.
Answer the questions.

Remember place value!

a. What is the <u>smallest</u> number you can make? _____

b. What is the <u>largest</u> number you can make? _____

c. What is the <u>largest</u> number you can make with the 2 in the hundreds place? _____

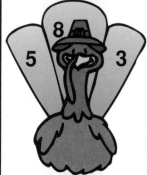

d. What is the <u>largest</u> number you can make? _____

e. What is the <u>smallest</u> number you can make? _____

f. What is the <u>smallest</u> number you can make with the 8 in the tens place? _____

g. What is the largest number you can make that is <u>less than 700</u>? _____

h. What number can you make that is <u>more than 847</u>? _____

i. What is the <u>largest</u> number you can make? _____

j. What are the three <u>largest</u> numbers you can make?

_____ _____ _____

k. What are the three <u>smallest</u> numbers you can make?

_____ _____ _____

Name_____

Having a Ball!

Use the balls to solve each problem below.
Write each answer in the blank.

1. Golfer Grant has 6 golf balls.
   If he shares them equally with two friends, how many golf balls will each player have? _____

2. Caddy Carl found 9 golf balls in a sand trap.
   If he divides them equally with two other friends, how many will each caddy have? _____

3. Greenskeeper Gertie bought a box of 12 golf balls.
   She and her two sisters will share them equally. How many golf balls will each sister get? _____

4. Three golfers show up to play a round of golf.
   They share a box of 18 balls so that each player gets the same amount. How many golf balls does each player get?
   _____

5. One day, Gary and Gabby Gopher found 14 golf balls.
   If they share them equally, how many golf balls will each gopher get? _____

6. The Pro Shop has 15 golf balls left after its big sale.
   If three people each buy the same amount, how many will each person buy? _____

7. Fairway Fran has 16 extra golf balls.
   If she gives each of 4 friends the same amount, how many will she give to each friend? _____

8. Hole-in-One Harry won 8 golf balls for having the best score.
   If he places them into 4 equal piles, how many golf balls will be in each pile? _____

At Home: Introduce your child to the concept of division by asking him or her to equally share a pile of pennies. Have him separate the pennies into equal sets for two, three, and four family members.

Underwater Wonders

Follow the directions.
Solve the problems.

1.

Make 2 rows.
Put 3 dots in each row.
2 x 3 = ___

2.

Make 5 rows.
Put 2 dots in each row.
5 x 2 = ___

4.

Make 3 rows.
Put 5 dots in each row.
3 x 5 = ___

3.

Make 3 rows.
Put 3 dots in each row.
3 x 3 = ___

5.

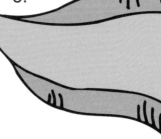

Try This: There are five fish in the fish tank.
Each fish has two eyes. How many fish eyes in
all? Write the multiplication sentence.

Make 2 rows.
Put 5 dots in each row.
2 x 5 = ___

Metric measurement

Long-Distance Friendship

Who has the longest long-distance friendship?
Use a ruler to draw lines and connect the dots.
Measure these lines in centimeters.
Write the measurements in the boxes below the lines.
Then add the measurements in each row, and write the totals in the blanks.

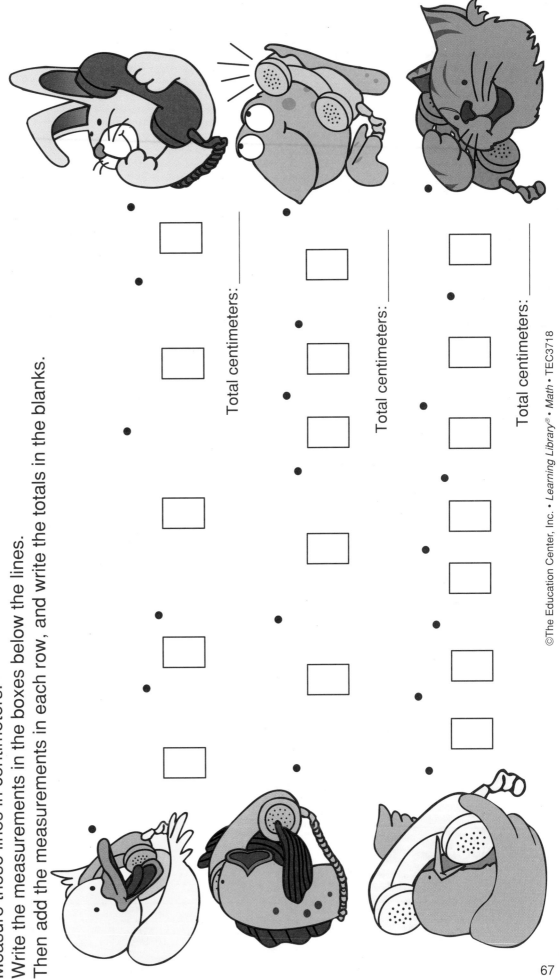

Total centimeters: _____

Total centimeters: _____

Total centimeters: _____

67

Name_____

Perimeter Pups

Perimeter is the distance around.

Measure each side.
Add the sides to find the *perimeter.*

1.

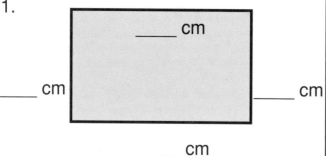

_____ cm

_____ cm   _____ cm

_____ cm

perimeter:

_____ + _____ + _____ + _____ = _____
                                    cm

2.

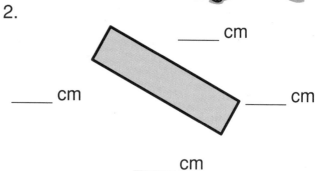

_____ cm

_____ cm   _____ cm

_____ cm

perimeter:

_____ + _____ + _____ + _____ = _____
                                    cm

3.

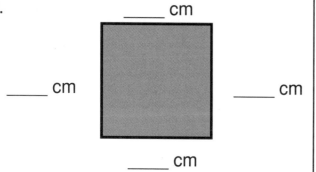

_____ cm

_____ cm   _____ cm

_____ cm

perimeter:

_____ + _____ + _____ + _____ = _____
                                    cm

4.

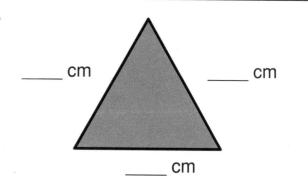

_____ cm   _____ cm

_____ cm

perimeter:

_____ + _____ + _____ = _____ cm

5.

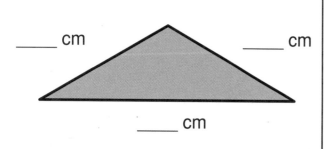

_____ cm   _____ cm

_____ cm

perimeter:

_____ + _____ + _____ = _____ cm

6.

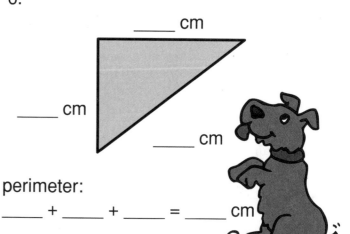

_____ cm

_____ cm

_____ cm

perimeter:

_____ + _____ + _____ = _____ cm

Try This: Can you find the perimeter of this page?

Name _____

How Do Frogs and Toads Measure Up?

Frogs and toads come in many different sizes.
Read about each frog or toad.
Then find an item that is the same length.
Write the name of the item on the line.

The paradoxical frog grows backwards! It shrinks from a large tadpole down to a 2-inch frog.

_____

The goliath frog is the largest of all frogs. This frog may grow to 12 inches long!

_____

The chirping frog makes a sound like a cricket's chirp. This frog can grow to $1\frac{1}{2}$ inches long.

_____

The Cuban arrow-poison frog is the smallest of all frogs. This frog only grows to about $\frac{1}{2}$ inch long!

_____

Leopard frogs have many spots! They can grow to 4 inches long.

_____

Bullfrogs take about 5 years to become adults. These frogs can grow to 8 inches long.

_____

The giant toad is one of the largest toads! It can grow to 9 inches long.

_____

Tree frogs are usually excellent jumpers. These tiny frogs only grow to about 1 inch long.

_____

The Surinam toad does not have a tongue! This unique frog can grow to 8 inches long.

_____

Which Way to Weigh?

It takes 16 ounces to make one pound.

This weighs about an <u>ounce</u>.

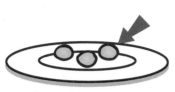

This weighs about a <u>pound</u>.

Look at the pictures.
Circle the best way to measure each object.

ounces
pounds

ounces
pounds

ounces
pounds

ounces
pounds

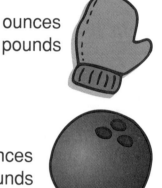

ounces
pounds

ounces
pounds

ounces
pounds

ounces
pounds

ounces
pounds

ounces
pounds

ounces
pounds

At Home: For practice with sorting and ordering, your child could help you put away the groceries or arrange cans by size.

Tip the Scales

I'm less than a pound!

Look at each picture.
Write *more* or *less* in each box.

A can of soup
weighs _____ than a pound.

A watermelon
weighs _____ than a pound.

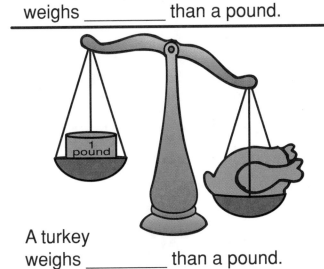

A turkey
weighs _____ than a pound.

An apple
weighs _____ than a pound.

A letter
weighs _____ than a pound.

A rabbit
weighs _____ than a pound.

Try This: Find three things that weigh about a pound each.

At Home: Check out the scales in the produce section of your local grocery store. Have your child tell whether he thinks one item of produce weighs more or less than another.

Weighty Matters

Look at each picture.
Circle the best
estimate for the
object.

1 pound
10 pounds

3 pounds
30 pounds

4 pounds
40 pounds

10 pounds
100 pounds

5 pounds
50 pounds

7 pounds
70 pounds

60 pounds
600 pounds

20 pounds
200 pounds

50 pound
500 pounds

8 pounds
80 pounds

At Home: Guess the tool! Ask your child, "If I wanted to measure ingredients for a cake, would I use a ruler or a cup?" or "What would I use to measure the weight of a puppy?"

Name_____

Fill 'er Up!

Look at the first picture in each row.
Then choose the best estimate.

1.

cup

less than a cup

more than a cup

2.

quart

less than a quart

more than a quart

3.

pint

less than a pint

more than a pint

4.

pint

less than a pint

more than a pint

5.

cup

less than a cup

more than a cup

Colorful Capacity

 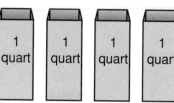 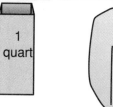

Quarts and gallons measure capacity.

4 quarts = 1 gallon

If the picture has about a one-quart capacity, color it blue.
If the picture has about a one-gallon capacity, color it red.

Cooking Oil

GAS

Apple Juice

At Home: Carpooling? Use the time in the car to teach the appropriate units used to measure different items. Ask your child to name things measured in inches, things that weigh about a pound (a loaf of bread, a jar of mustard, a blow dryer), or things you would not measure by the cup (shampoo, toothpaste, gasoline).

©The Education Center, Inc. • *Learning Library*® • *Math* • TEC3718

Name_____

Celsius Seasons

Read the date below each thermometer.
Find the information on the chart.
Color in the thermometer to match.
Then use the code to outline each
    thermometer.

hot = red   cool = green
warm = orange   cold = blue

Date	Temperature	Weather
January 3	6°C	cold
February 17	8°C	cold
March 9	18°C	cool
May 21	28°C	warm
June 10	32°C	warm
August 23	40°C	hot
September 16	26°C	warm
October 28	20°C	cool

1.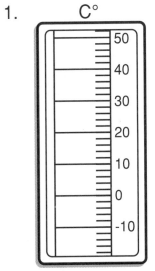
September 16

2.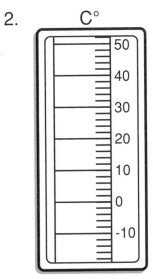
June 10

3.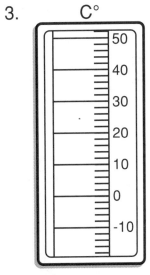
February 17

4.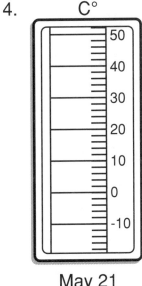
May 21

5.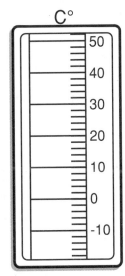
October 28

6.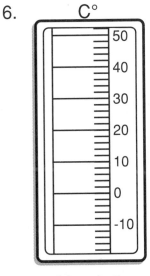
March 9

7.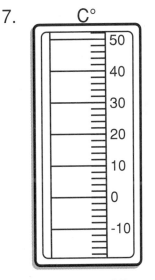
August 23

8.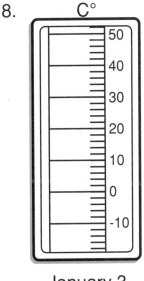
January 3

Name_____

Frogtown's Helpful Weatherfrog

In the springtime, Frogtown's temperatures change daily.
Write each temperature shown.

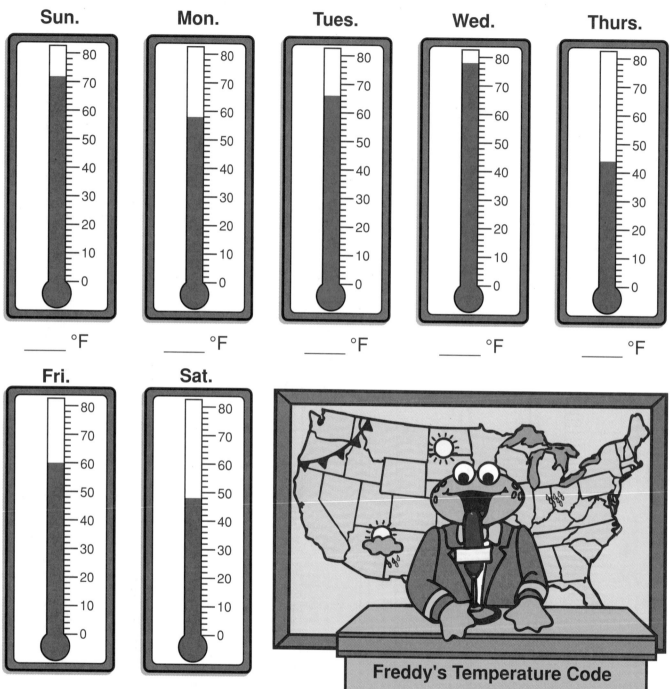

Sun.	Mon.	Tues.	Wed.	Thurs.
____ °F	____ °F	____ °F	____ °F	____ °F

Fri.	Sat.
____ °F	____ °F

The frogs listen to the daily
  forecast to know what to wear.
Show what the weatherfrog
  told them to wear each day
  this week.
Use the code.

Freddy's Temperature Code

70° and above—shorts & T-shirts
Circle these temperatures.

50°–69°—jacket
Underline these temperatures.

49° and below—hat and gloves
Box these temperatures.

Name_____

Let's Review

Write the fraction for the shaded part.

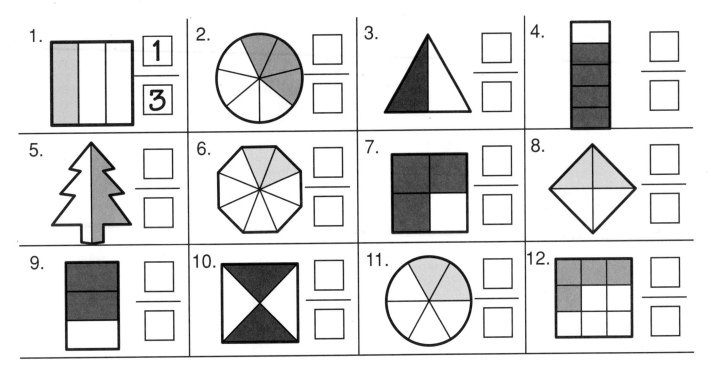

1. [1] [3]

2.

3.

4.

5.

6.

7.

8.

9.

10.

11.

12.

Draw lines to show what tool you would use to measure.

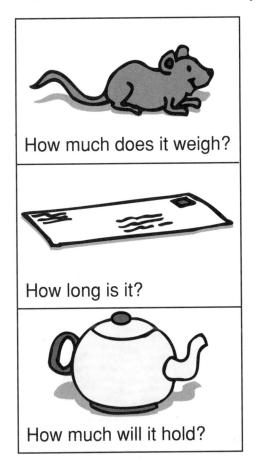

How much does it weigh?

How long is it?

How much will it hold?

Now go to the next page and show what you know.

Let's Review, Too!

Shade to show the fraction amount.

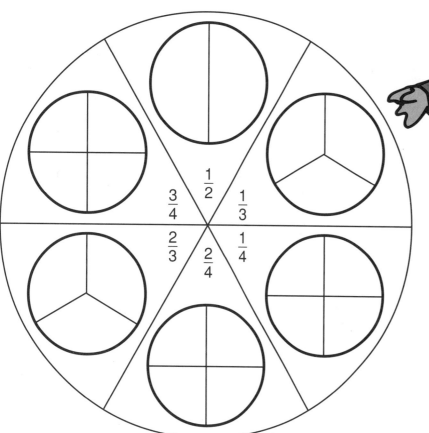

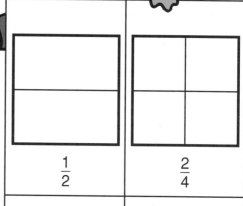

$\frac{1}{2}$ $\frac{2}{4}$

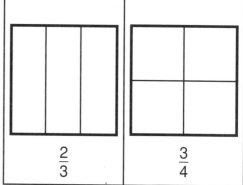

$\frac{2}{3}$ $\frac{3}{4}$

Write to tell what each tool measures.
Use the word box.

Word Box
weight
length
capacity
temperature

You will use some words more than once.

Time and Money

This year your child will go beyond reading a clock. He will learn relationships of time: determining A.M. and P.M., the minutes in an hour, the days in a week, the months in the year. He'll be able to describe activities that take one second, one minute, and one hour.

Children in second grade use both *analog* and *digital* clocks to tell time using hours and minutes and five-minute intervals. Make sure your child has opportunities to use both types of clocks at home. Your child will be able to use his understanding of *elapsed time* to solve word problems (for example, "The movie starts at 2:30 P.M. We get out of the show at 4:00 P.M. How long did the movie last?"). It's time to invest in an inexpensive wristwatch for your child!

When working with money, second graders recognize and count pennies, nickels, dimes, quarters, half-dollars, and dollar bills. In school, they practice finding the value of a set of coins less than one dollar, creating given amounts with the fewest coins, and comparing coin amounts to prices. They learn to solve problems involving money and to write money amounts using the decimal point and dollar sign. In addition, second graders begin to make change. This skill takes lots of practice, so be prepared to help him make purchases and count back the change together.

Your second grader should be able to
- read a calendar comparing periods of time such as 3 weeks to 19 days
- tell time to the hour, half hour, and quarter hour
- solve problems involving elapsed time
- count coin combinations up to 50 cents, starting with the coin with the greatest value
- make change for $1.00
- compare prices to money amounts
- write money amounts with decimal point and dollar sign
- solve word problems involving money.

Key Math Skills for Grade 2
Time and Money

Time: minutes in an hour, days in a week, months in a year

Time: using a calendar (for example, "Which is longer: 3 weeks or 19 days?")

Time: sequencing events and determining *early* or *late* (for example, "The play starts at 3:15. Sam arrives at 3:20. Is Sam early or late?")

Time: telling time to the hour, half hour, and quarter hour

Time: elapsed time (for example, "Joe arrives at the party at 2:00. He leaves two hours later. What time did Joe leave?")

Money: counting combinations of coins to make an amount with the fewest coins

Money: comparing coin combinations to prices

Money: making change for $1.00

Word problems: solving problems with money

Money: using decimal notation

Colorful Calendar

Follow the directions to color the calendar.

JUNE

Sun.	Mon.	Tues.	Wed.	Thurs.	Fri.	Sat.
				1	2	3
4	5	6	7	8	9	10
11	12	13	14	15	16	17
18	19	20	21	22	23	24
25	26	27	28	29	30	

1. Draw a blue circle around the first day of the month.

2. What day is the first day on? _____

3. Draw a green △ on June 22.

4. Draw a yellow ✿ on each day of the last week.

5. Draw a red ☐ on the second Saturday.

6. Draw a purple X on the first Saturday.

7. Draw a brown ◇ on June 16.

8. Draw a black → on the day that July will begin.

At Home: If you have a calendar, then it's easy to reinforce time concepts with your child. Ask a daily calendar question such as "How many days are there until we visit Grandma?" or "Which is longer: two weeks or 13 days?" You'll be surprised at how a daily dose of questioning will build calendar connections!

Mouse's Month

Use the calendar to answer the questions.

March						
Sun.	**Mon.**	**Tues.**	**Wed.**	**Thurs.**	**Fri.**	**Sat.**
			1	2	3	4
5	6	7	8	9	10	11
12	13	14	15	16	17	18
19	20	21	22	23	24	25
26	27	28	29	30	31	

1. Mouse is going to the cheese festival on March 20. If he comes home a week later, what will the date be?

   _____

2. On March 3, Mouse's friend calls to say she will come visit in two weeks. On what date will she visit?

   _____

3. Mouse cleans house once a week. If he cleaned on the first Sunday, on what date will he clean again?

   _____

4. Mouse gets his tail washed and curled every Thursday. How many times will he get his tail washed in March? _____

5. Mouse has a cheeseburger every Monday and Wednesday. How many will he have this month? _____

6. Mouse looked at his calendar to see how many full weeks are in March. How many are there?

   _____

7. On March 5, Mouse noticed it was only three weeks until his birthday. What date is his birthday?

   _____

8. A letter was mailed to Mouse on March 17. If he got it a week later, what was the date? _____

9. Mouse will go camping on the last day of the month. What day of the week will that be? _____

10. Mouse will buy a tent the Sunday before he goes camping. What date will that be? _____

Name ____________________

It's Pizza Time!

Read each clock.
Write the time below it.

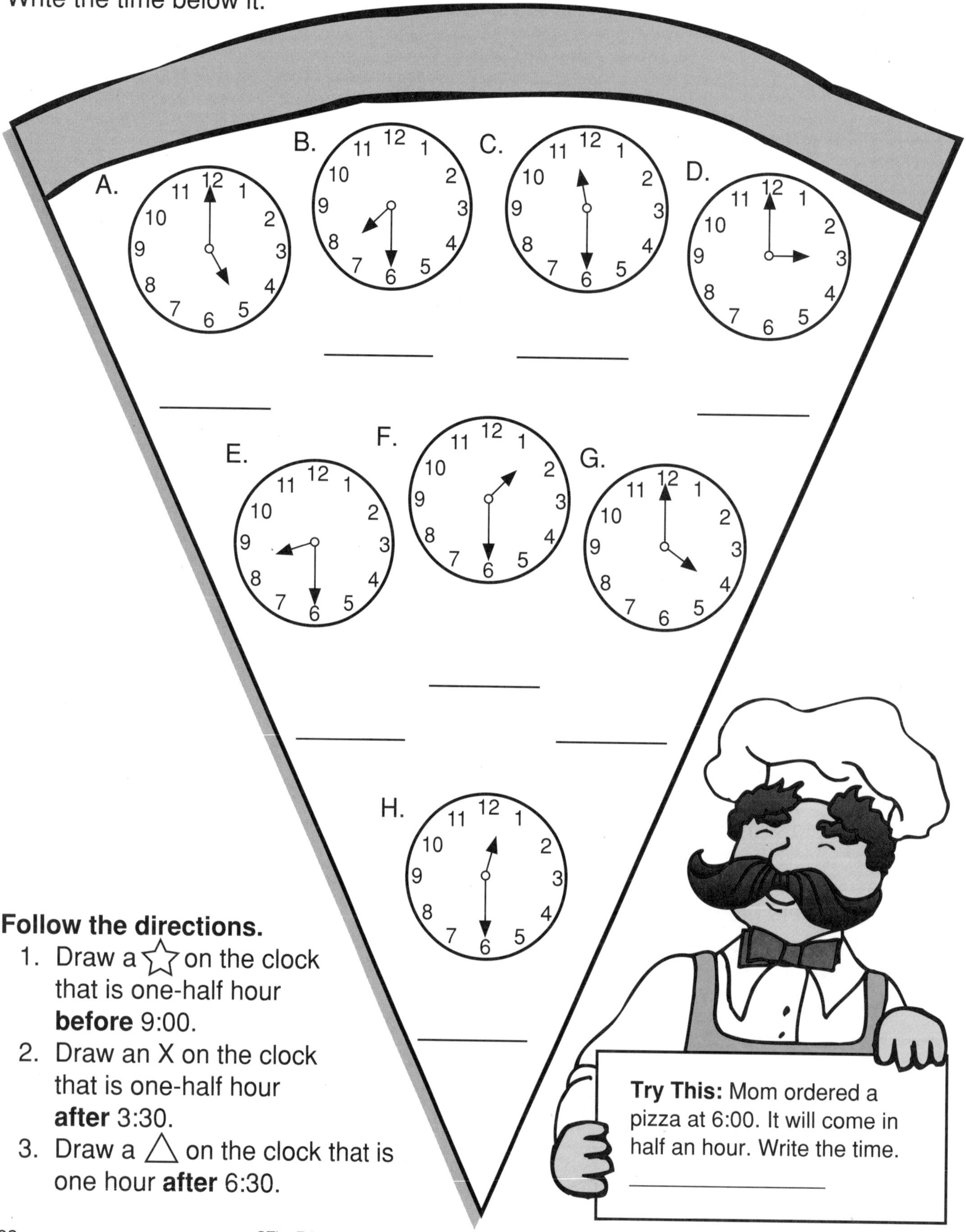

Follow the directions.

1. Draw a ☆ on the clock that is one-half hour **before** 9:00.
2. Draw an X on the clock that is one-half hour **after** 3:30.
3. Draw a △ on the clock that is one hour **after** 6:30.

Try This: Mom ordered a pizza at 6:00. It will come in half an hour. Write the time.

____

Name _____

Time for a Snack

Count by 5s.
Write the time on the lines below each clock.
Color the cheese holes yellow as you use the answers.

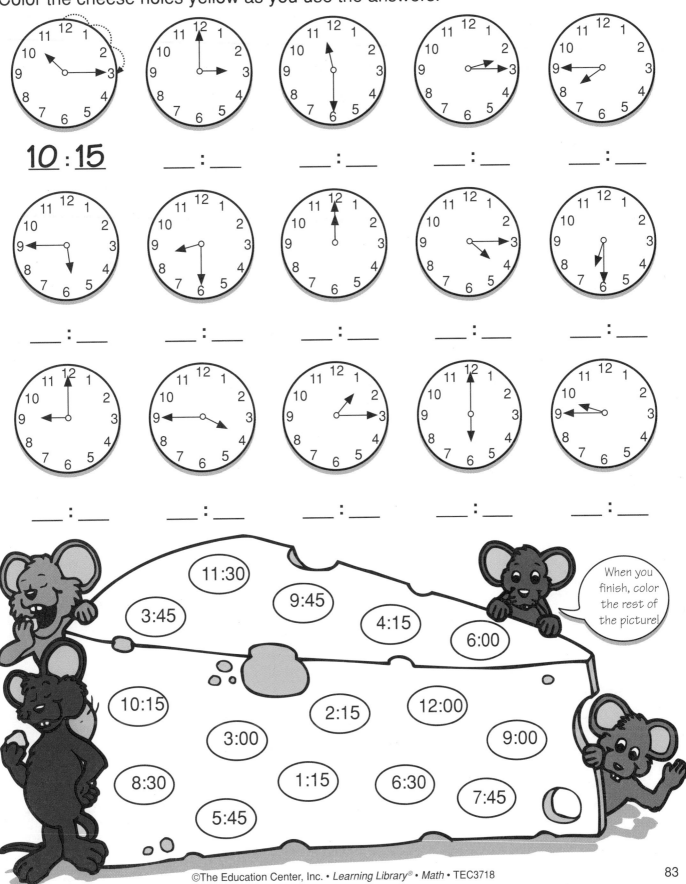

10 : 15

___ : ___

___ : ___

___ : ___

___ : ___

___ : ___

___ : ___

___ : ___

___ : ___

___ : ___

___ : ___

___ : ___

___ : ___

___ : ___

___ : ___

11:30

9:45

3:45

4:15

6:00

10:15

2:15

12:00

3:00

9:00

8:30

1:15

6:30

7:45

5:45

When you finish, color the rest of the picture!

©The Education Center, Inc. • Learning Library® • Math • TEC3718

83

Name _____

Time to Go!

When Mr. Ratburn's class goes to Washington, DC,
  they have a very busy schedule.
Write the time shown on each clock.
Then write a numeral in each star to show the
  correct order.

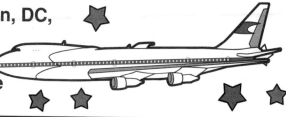

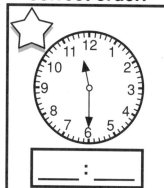

The class sees
the Washington
Monument.

_____ : _____

Arthur gives
his speech.

_____ : _____

Then Arthur and
his friends go to
the White House.

_____ : _____

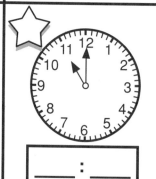

Everyone meets
at the Jefferson
Memorial on
Wednesday
morning.

_____ : _____

The next stop is
the Capitol.

_____ : _____

The president
arrives in a
helicopter.

_____ : _____

Read each question.
Write the answer on the line.

A. After the class saw the Washington Monument, how many minutes later did they
   visit the Capitol? _____

B. Arthur arrived at the White House at 12:00. How many minutes later did he give
   his speech? _____

84   ©The Education Center, Inc. • Learning Library® • Math • TEC3718

Name _____

Frozen in Time

Read each clock.
Color the two ice cubes with matching times.

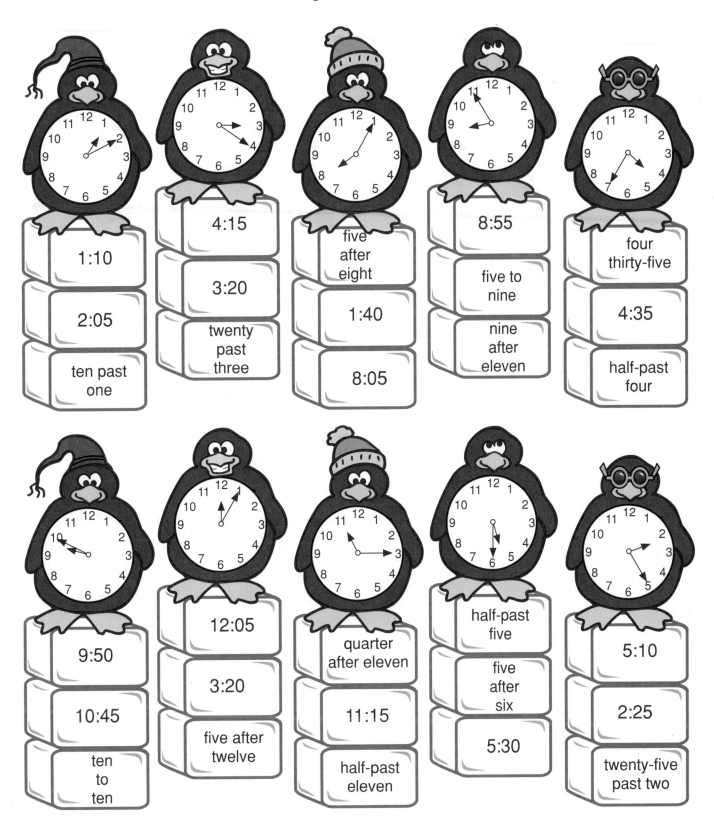

1:10

2:05

ten past
one

4:15

3:20

twenty
past
three

five
after
eight

1:40

8:05

8:55

five to
nine

nine
after
eleven

four
thirty-five

4:35

half-past
four

9:50

10:45

ten
to
ten

12:05

3:20

five after
twelve

quarter
after eleven

11:15

half-past
eleven

half-past
five

five
after
six

5:30

5:10

2:25

twenty-five
past two

85

Changing Times

Write the times.
Circle A.M. or P.M.

1. School starts.

A.M.
P.M.

5 minutes later

2. School is over.

A.M.
P.M.

5 minutes later

3. Eat breakfast.
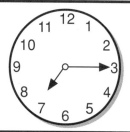
A.M.
P.M.

10 minutes later

4. Do homework.

A.M.
P.M.

10 minutes later

5. Time to wake up.

A.M.
P.M.

15 minutes later

6. Get ready for bed.
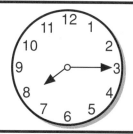
A.M.
P.M.

15 minutes later

At Home: Help your child develop a sense of time passage with this simple activity. Set the timer for one minute and see how many times your child can tie his shoes, recite a poem, or touch his toes. Or make the activity more productive by seeing how many toys he can pick up, how many pair of socks he can find mates for, or how many dishes he can wash!

©The Education Center, Inc. • *Learning Library*® • *Math* • TEC3718

Time After Time

Read each time.
Write it on each set of clocks.

| one thirty | five after five | seven o'clock | nine fifteen | quarter to four |

Show the time one hour later.

| 8:00 | 4:30 | 6:15 | 2:45 | 11:20 |

Number each face clock.
Show the time.

When I wake up

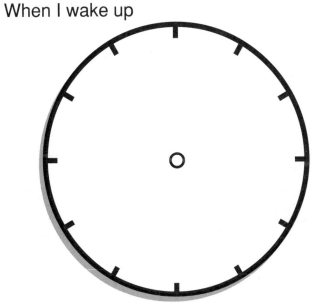

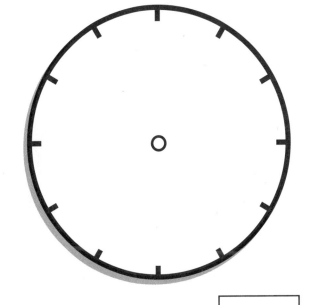

When I go to bed

Name _____

Pigs in a Blanket

Count the coins on each piggy's blanket.
Write the amount in the blank.
In each pair, color the piggy's blanket
  that shows more money.

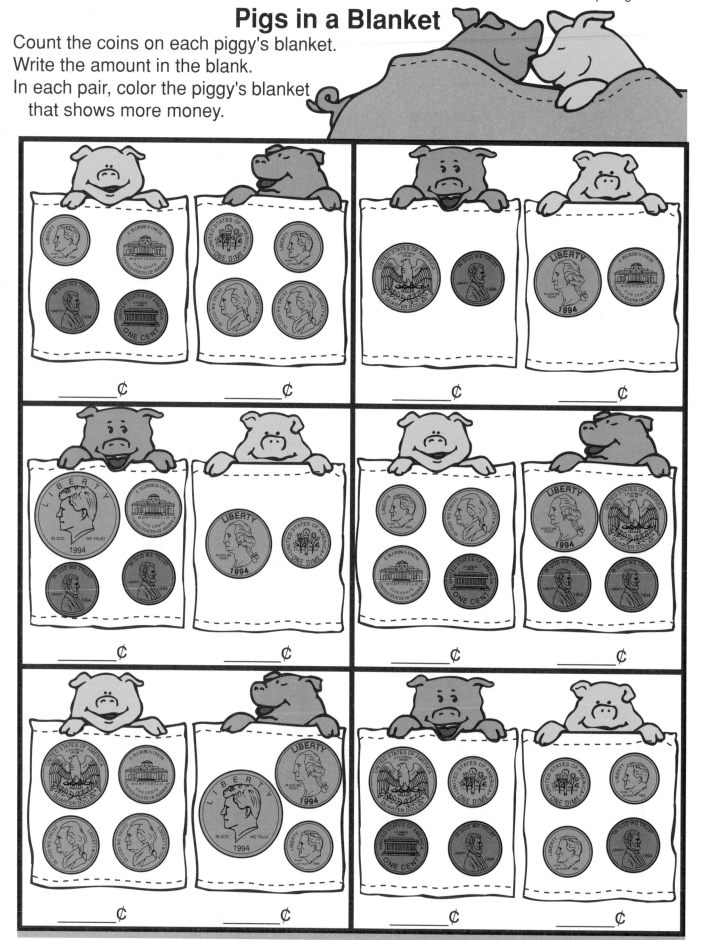

_____ ¢   _____ ¢

_____ ¢   _____ ¢

_____ ¢   _____ ¢

_____ ¢   _____ ¢

_____ ¢   _____ ¢

_____ ¢   _____ ¢

Name _____

Put It in the Bank

Color the coins needed to fill each piggy bank.

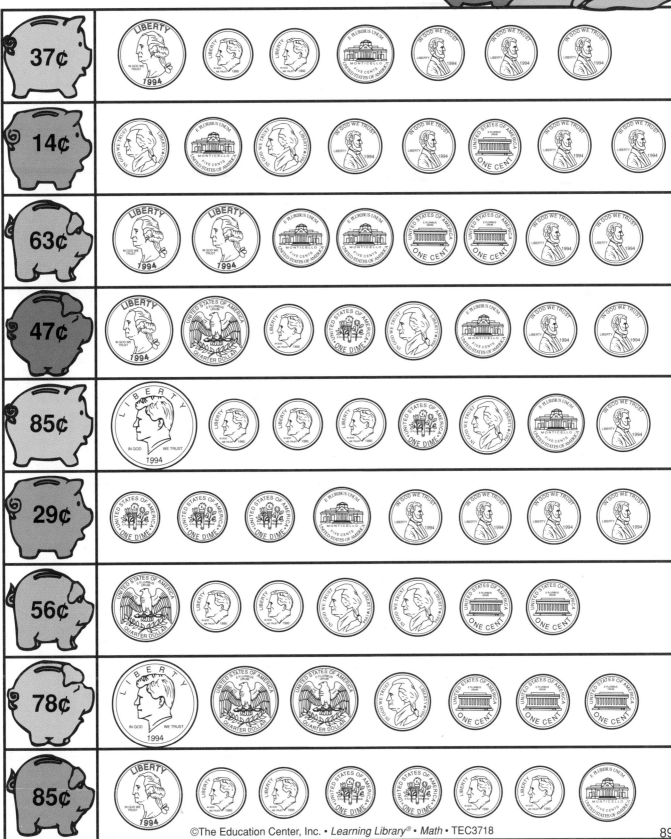

Piggy's Popcorn Shop

In each box, circle the coins needed to buy the flavor of popcorn.

Popcorn Shop			
Popcorn Shop			
10 delicious flavors			
plain 50		sour cream 88	
butter 54		peanutty 98	
cheese...................... 62		chili 75	
caramel 78		nacho 64	
barbeque 66		maple 83	

butter

cheese

peanutty

maple

caramel

nacho

chili

sour cream

barbeque

90   ©The Education Center, Inc. • *Learning Library®* • Math • TEC3718

Coin Count

Show how many coins to make the amount.
Choose the fewest number of coins.
Use real coins to help if needed.

Amount	quarters	dimes	nickels	pennies
35¢				
24¢				
40¢				
60¢				
51¢				
32¢				
15¢				
25¢				
70¢				
38¢				
20¢				
14¢				
47¢				

At Home: Bring the piggy bank into play to review coin combinations. Your child should be able to count a mixed collection of coins to 99 cents. Challenge him to count a total of 50 cents using at least three different coin combinations. Then count out another amount and have him match it using a different combination of coins.

Name _____

Chauncey's Change Purses

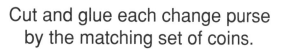

Cut and glue each change purse
by the matching set of coins.

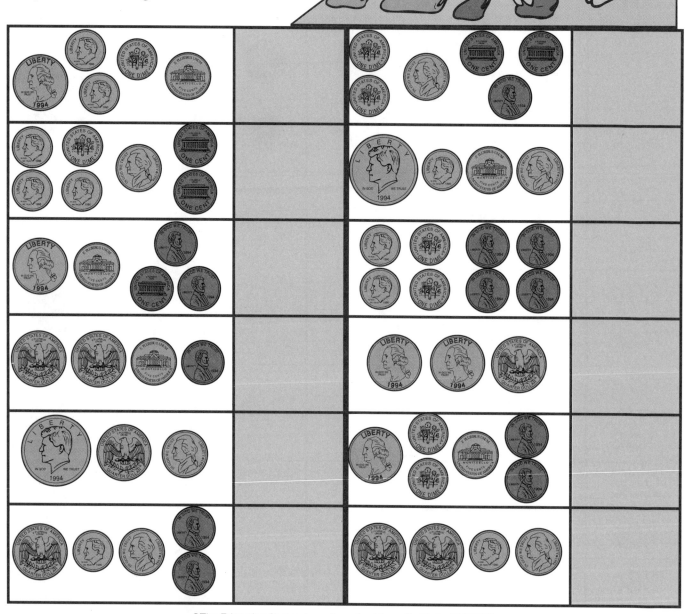

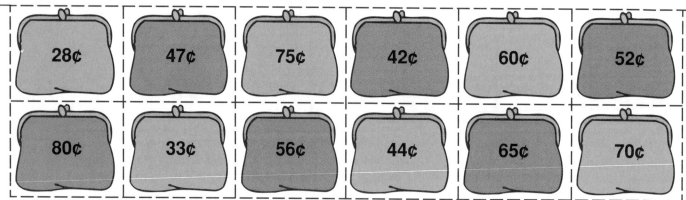

28¢ 47¢ 75¢ 42¢ 60¢ 52¢

80¢ 33¢ 56¢ 44¢ 65¢ 70¢

Percy's Purchases

Read each problem and answer the question.

1. Percy bought a candy bar for 35 cents and a soda for 62 cents. How much did he spend in all? _____

2. Lollipops cost 25 cents each. How much will it cost if Percy buys three of them?

_____

3. Percy counted the money left in his pockets. He has 50 cents in one pocket and 46 cents in the other pocket. How much money does Percy have left? _____

4. An ice cream cone costs 98 cents. Does Percy have enough to buy one? _____

5. A pack of gum costs 24 cents. Percy gave the clerk two dimes. How much more does he need to give him?

_____

6. Percy wants to buy peppermints for his sister. If they cost 5 cents each, how many can he get with a quarter? _____

7. Percy has four dimes, one nickel, and two pennies left. How much is that in all? _____

8. On the way home, Percy found a dime. How much money does he have now?

_____

At Home: Making change can be a difficult task for second-grade students. Your child will gain an advantage if you provide opportunities for him to pay for small purchases and count the change he gets back. Once he becomes confident with this, have him determine how much money he should receive in change before he makes the purchase. Then have him count the change to confirm his answer.

Presto Change-o!

For each purchase, figure the change due.
The first one is done for you.

---

1. I have .

I spent 22¢.

$$\begin{array}{r} 25¢ \\ -\ 22¢ \\ \hline 3¢ \end{array}$$

My change is:

---

2. I have .

I spent 25¢.

$$\begin{array}{r} \underline{\quad}¢ \\ -\ 25¢ \\ \hline ¢ \end{array}$$

My change is:

---

3. I have .

I spent 28¢.

$$\begin{array}{r} \underline{\quad}¢ \\ -\ 28¢ \\ \hline ¢ \end{array}$$

My change is:

---

4. I have .

I spent 35¢.

$$\begin{array}{r} \underline{\quad}¢ \\ -\ 35¢ \\ \hline ¢ \end{array}$$

My change is:

---

5. I have .

I spent 60¢.

$$\begin{array}{r} \underline{\quad}¢ \\ -\ 60¢ \\ \hline ¢ \end{array}$$

My change is:

---

6. I have  .

I spent 35¢.

$$\begin{array}{r} \underline{\quad}¢ \\ -\ 35¢ \\ \hline ¢ \end{array}$$

My change is:

---

7. I have .

I spent 23¢.

$$\begin{array}{r} \underline{\quad}¢ \\ -\ 23¢ \\ \hline ¢ \end{array}$$

My change is:

---

8. I have .

I spent 37¢.

$$\begin{array}{r} \underline{\quad}¢ \\ -\ 37¢ \\ \hline ¢ \end{array}$$

My change is:

Bank on It!

Write how much money.

1.

_____¢

2.

_____¢

Count the coins.
Circle the answer.

3.

Can you buy it?

yes

no

_____¢

4.

Can you buy it?

yes

no

_____¢

How much change back?

5. You have

You buy
25¢

How much change back?

How much change back?

6. You have

You buy
31¢

How much change back?

---

7. Add.
   2 dimes + 2 nickels = _____¢

8.
   1 quarter + 4 pennies = _____¢

Geometry

In second grade, your child will explore the world of shapes and the results of moving, flipping, or turning shapes. He will be asked to name, draw, and build both two-dimensional and three-dimensional geometric figures. He'll be able to describe how two shapes or two solids are alike and how they are different, comparing numbers of sides and corners.

Second graders are introduced to new words such as *congruent* (figures having the same size and shape), *symmetry* (made by folding along a line so that two parts match exactly) and *transformations* (rotating or flipping the position of a figure).

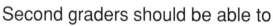

Help your child see geometric shapes in art, architecture, and all around him in his environment. If your child is familiar with geometry vocabulary and concepts, he will be more comfortable using his knowledge to solve problems and participate in class.

Second graders should be able to
- identify and compare *plane* (two-dimensional) and *solid* (three-dimensional) geometric shapes
- sort plane figures by size, color, shape, number of sides or corners
- compare and sort solid figures, counting the number of *faces* or edges
- make *symmetrical* shapes by cutting and folding paper or painting
- identify and combine congruent figures
- recognize and apply *transformations* (flipping, sliding, or turning shapes)
- recognize geometric shapes and structures in the environment

Key Math Skills for Grade 2
Geometry

- Plane figures: identifying, comparing and sorting *plane* (two-dimensional) *figures* such as rectangles, squares, circles, ovals, and triangles

- Solid figures: identifying, comparing, and sorting solid shapes such as spheres, cubes, cylinders, pyramids, and rectangular prisms according to number of faces, edges, or *vertices*

- Combining and taking apart shapes (for example, separating and combining shapes to make new figures using *tangrams*)

- Identifying *congruent* figures

- Identifying and creating symmetry using paper cutting, folding, or mirrors

- Recognizing and applying *slides, flips,* and *turns* (for example, manipulating real objects or objects on a computer 180 degrees)

- Recognizing shapes from different perspectives

- Recognizing geometric shapes and structures in the environment

Out on the Town

As you travel in the car or walk together, ask your child to point out different shapes in the buildings and structures around you. Windows, for example, might be shaped like squares, rectangles, or even circles. If the windows are divided into equal parts, ask your child to name the shapes of the sections.

Once your child is proficient at naming shapes, pose a more challenging task: select a building and have your child try to find at least five different shapes within the structure.

Shape Sort

Make a display of some household items such as an eraser, a box of raisins, a can of vegetables, a party hat, a baseball, a cereal box, a soft drink can, an orange, and a funnel. Ask your child to sort the objects by shape. Then, as an added challenge, have her think of a different way to sort the objects. Reinforce the word *attribute* as a word for describing things about an object.

Shape Sort

Meet the Shape family.

Tim
Triangle

Rita
Rhombus

Cindy
Circle

Robert
Rectangle

Sam
Square

Olivia
Oval

Draw the shapes that belong in each group.

Shapes With 4 Sides	Blue Shapes
Shapes With 3 Sides	**Shapes That Are Not Blue**
Round Shapes	**Shapes That Do Not Have 4 Sides**

Name_____

Shape Up!

In each box, color the shapes that belong in the group.

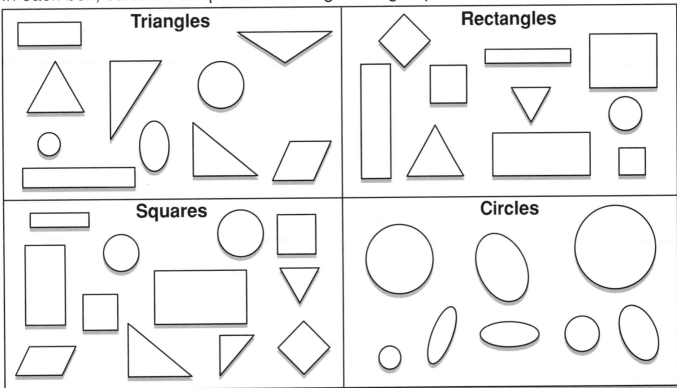

Draw 4 shapes in each box. Make each shape unlike the others.

Rectangles	Squares
Circles	**Triangles**

Name_____

Swine-Mart Sort

Help Petey and Petra Pig sort their groceries by shape.
Cut out the boxes.
Glue them next to the correct grocery bags.

Cylinders				
Cubes				
Spheres				
Rectangular Prisms				

At Home: When grocery shopping together, look for cylinders, pyramids, rectangular prisms, cubes, and spheres.

©The Education Center, Inc. • *Learning Library*® • *Math* • TEC3718

100

Shapes All Around

Solid figures have **faces** that look like plane shapes.
Match the solid figure to its face, or plane shape.

Your face looks familiar!

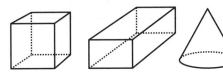

Many solids have faces, edges, and corners.

Edges are the lines where 2 faces meet.

Faces are flat.

Corners are where edges meet.

Follow the directions for each solid figure.

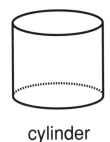 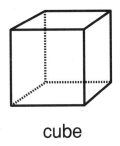 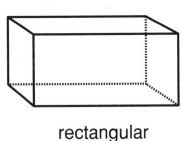  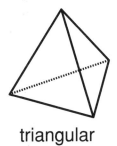

cube   cylinder   rectangular prism   cone   triangular prism

1. Trace the **edges** of the cube with green crayon.

2. Color the **face** of the cylinder red.

3. Circle the **corners** of the rectangular prism.

4. Color the **face** of the cone blue.

5. Count the **corners** of the triangular prism. ____ corners

Try This: Try to find each type of solid figure in your kitchen.

Shape Study

Symmetrical figures can be divided into two parts that are mirror images.

Congruent figures have the same size and shape.

 A circle is symmetrical.

These rectangles are congruent.

Make each figure symmetrical.

1.

2.

3.
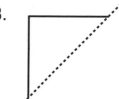

4.

Draw a line of symmetry to divide each figure.

5.
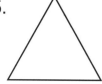

6.

7.
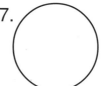

8.

Draw a figure that is congruent.

9.

10.
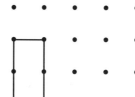

11.
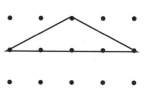

12.
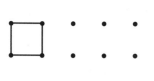

13.
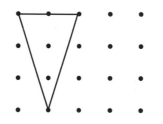

14.
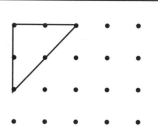

At Home: Help your child look through discarded magazines and newspapers to find pictures of objects that are symmetrical. Once she identifies a symmetrical object, have her cut it out and fold it in half to test for the line of symmetry.

©The Education Center, Inc. • *Learning Library® • Math* • TEC3718

Head Over Heels!

1. A **flip** makes a figure face the other way.
   Flip these figures. The first one is done for you.

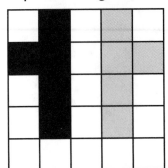 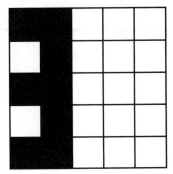 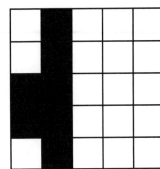 

1. A **turn** makes a figure rotate.
   Turn these figures.

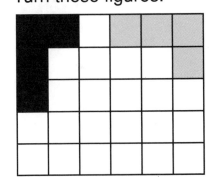 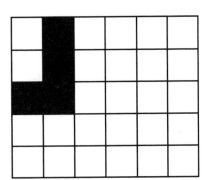 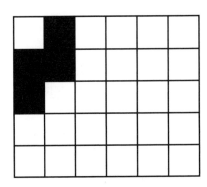

3. A **slide** moves a figure up, down, or sideways without turning or flipping.
   Slide the triangle in each pattern.

○△○   ○ △○   ○○△○   □○△□

3. Follow the directions.

Flip.   Slide.   Turn.

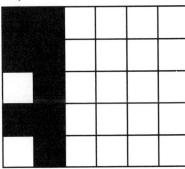   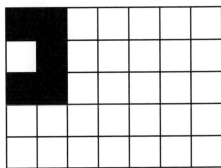

It Figures!

1. How many squares are in this rectangle? _____

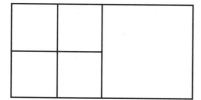

Hint: Trace over each square as you count.

2. How many squares are in this triangle? _____

   How many triangles? _____

   How many rectangles? _____

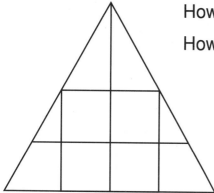

3. Draw a shape that is congruent.
   Then draw a line of symmetry.

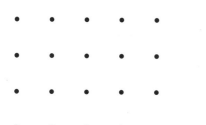

4. Color one of the faces on each figure.
   Trace the edges.
   Circle the corners.

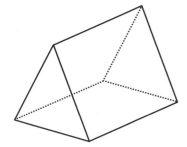  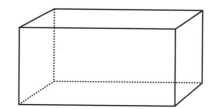 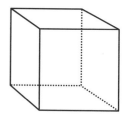

Patterns, Functions, and Algebra

Patterns of shapes and numbers are found in nature, in art, in music, and in the rhythms of life. When children count by twos, threes, or fives, they are creating patterns too. Understanding that there are patterns in numbers will help your child compare numbers and remember basic addition, subtraction, and multiplication facts. To help your child see number patterns, have him create a *hundreds chart* with ten rows and ten columns, and ask him to find patterns in the numbers. For example, count by tens starting with 28, 38, and 48. Ask, "What comes next?"

Your second grader will practice sorting, classifying, and ordering objects by size and shape. Then he'll try repeating or extending patterns and determining what should come next or what is left out of a series. You can discover together how *growing patterns* are produced (for example, ask, "How many legs do two spiders have? How about three spiders? Four spiders?").

Second graders create *function tables* to show what happens to numbers when a certain operation is performed on all numbers in the table, such as adding 4. These charts help children see the relationships between numbers and prompt them to write number sentences such as x + 4 = ___. Looks like algebra? It is! Second graders will learn that changes can be represented using symbols and equations.

Second graders can
- complete charts that show a *function*, such as adding 4
- write number sentences with symbols such as +, −, and =
- sort, classify, and order objects by shape and size
- recognize and extend patterns of shapes or numbers
- skip-count by twos, threes, fives, and tens to 100
- identify even and odd numbers

Key Math Skills for Grade 2
Patterns, Functions, and Algebra

Patterns: ordering objects by size, number, and other properties

Patterns: recognizing and extending patterns such as sequences of shapes or simple numbers (for example, "What comes next?" "How can the pattern be repeated or extended?")

Patterns: understanding repeating and growing patterns (for example, finding the number of ears on one horse, two horses, and three horses.)

Patterns: using skip-counting on a hundreds chart (for example, "If you count by tens beginning with 36, what number would you count next?")

Patterns: skip-counting by twos, threes, fives, and tens

Patterns: identifying even and odd numbers

Algebra: using symbols (+, −, =, x, -) to write number sentences

Algebra: using the equal sign for equivalent relationships

Functions: completing function tables

Functions: modeling subtraction, multiplication and division using objects and pictures to solve problems

Who's Got the Button?

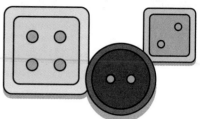

Find the pattern in each row.

Finish the row.

1.   _____

2.   _____

3.   _____

4.   _____

5.   _____

6.   _____

7.   _____

At Home: Use an assortment of coins or pieces of dry pasta shapes to create a pattern. Ask your child to continue the pattern a specific amount of places. Make sure you vary the patterning sequence so that you reinforce patterns such as ABAB, ABBA, ABCABC, etc. Then have your child create a pattern for you to extend.

Name_____

Pattern Puzzlers

Draw to complete each pattern.
Then count the shapes.

1.   _____ _____ _____

   How many triangles in all? _____

2. 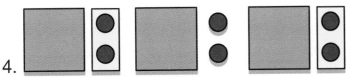   _____ _____ _____

   How many squares in all? _____

3. 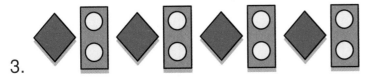   _____ _____ _____

   How many circles in all? _____

4. 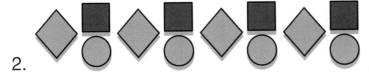   _____ _____ _____

   How many rectangles in all? _____

5. 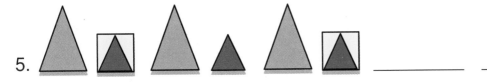   _____ _____ _____

   How many triangles in all? _____

6. 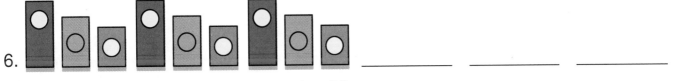   _____ _____ _____

   How many circles and rectangles in all? _____

At Home: Together look for patterns that are repeated in wallpaper or fabric. Have your child draw on paper with crayons or markers to reproduce the pattern.

Nutty Numbers

Complete the chart.
Then follow the directions.

1	2	3	4						
			14			17			
			24	25	26				
		33							
	42			45					
		53						59	
61						67			
					76				
		83							
91							98		

1. Make a green X on each odd number.

2. Count by 2s. Color each box yellow.

3. Count by 5s. Trace around each box in blue.

4. Count by 10s. Put a red dot in each box.

5. Complete: 14, 16, 18, ___, ___, 24, ___, ___, ___

6. Complete: 35, 40, 45, ___, ___, ___, 65, ___, ___

7. Complete: 100, 90, 80, ___, ___, ___, ___, ___, 20

At Home: Ask your child to count aloud by tens to 100 as he writes the numbers on a sheet of paper. Have him identify any patterns he sees on the page. Then challenge him to count by tens, starting at 11 and stopping at 91. Help him recognize patterns in the sequence of written numbers. Try the activity several more times, starting at 14 and stopping at 94, and starting at 17 and stopping at 97. Be sure to have your child look for the number patterns each time.

Don't Tip the Scales!

Make each scale balance with a number to make it equal.

1. $\underline{5} + \underline{5} = \underline{3} + \underline{}$

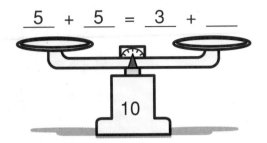

2. $\underline{2} + \underline{8} = \underline{6} + \underline{}$

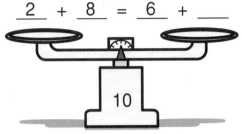

3. $\underline{7} + \underline{8} = \underline{9} + \underline{}$

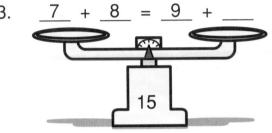

4. $\underline{4} + \underline{11} = \underline{5} + \underline{}$

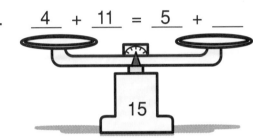

5. $\underline{12} + \underline{8} = \underline{13} + \underline{}$

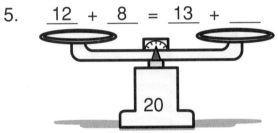

6. $\underline{15} + \underline{5} = \underline{17} + \underline{}$

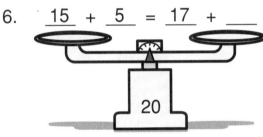

On each scale, circle = if the sums are equal or ≠ if the sums are not equal.

7. 14 + 5   16 + 4

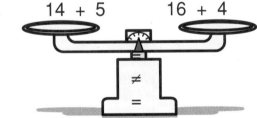

8. 7 + 6   4 + 9

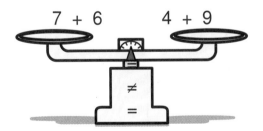

9. 10 + 7   9 + 6

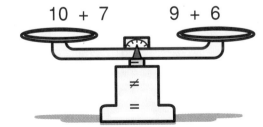

10. 12 + 6   9 + 9

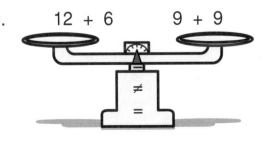

What's My Rule?

Read each rule.
Write the missing numbers.

Rule: Add 4	
4	
7	
9	
6	

Rule: Add 8	
6	
8	
9	
5	

Now look at each function table.
Tell the rule.

Rule: Add ___	
9	11
7	
5	
8	10

Rule: Add ___	
5	10
11	
7	12
6	

Rule: Add ___	
6	
9	15
10	
4	

Rule: Add ___	
12	15
10	
5	
8	

Write the missing numbers.

Rule: Doubles	
7	14
4	
6	
9	

Rule: Make 12	
8	4
10	
3	
5	

Rule: Subtract 7	
18	11
12	
17	
19	

Rule: Add 10	
5	15
9	
12	
14	

Try This: Draw a function table. Write a rule at the top such as "Subtract 9." Have someone fill in the numbers on one side. Complete the table.

Graphing, Probability, and Problem Solving

In second grade, your child will learn to read an assortment of graphs such as picture graphs and bar graphs. Your child will be able to

- take a survey to gather data
- record data using tally marks
- organize and display information in a graph
- draw conclusions and answer questions based on graphs

Your child will explore probability. You may be thinking, "Weather predictions and economic forecasts involve probability, but what's that got to do with second grade?" It's because your child is beginning to understand that some events are predictable. When your child plays a game that uses a spinner or dice, probability is involved. Your second-grader will begin to use basic concepts of probability, such as

- recognizing that some events are predictable
- determining if events are certain or impossible
- predicting possible outcomes of games with spinners and dice

You can help your child see math problems as fun! Show her how you use math to solve everyday problems—to make decisions such as how to spend money on purchases, how much time to allow for getting to work or school, when to schedule car maintenance, or when to fill up the gas tank.

Let your child know that there may be more than one way to solve a problem. Allow her to decide if one or more of these problem-solving strategies are appropriate: drawing a picture, building a model, acting it out, making a list, working backward, estimating the answer, guessing and checking.

Key Math Skills for Grade 2
Graphing, Probability, and Problem Solving

- Gathering information (data) about self and surroundings using counts, tallies, and surveys
- Graphing: organizing and displaying data using counts, tallies, tables, and bar graphs
- Graphing: selecting appropriate methods to represent data
- Graphing: describing parts of the data and the data as a whole (for example, "Whom do I count? How can I be sure I counted each piece of data only once? What is a good title for my survey results?")
- Graphing: understanding that the results from one sample may not apply to another sample
- Probability: understanding events as certain or impossible, most likely or least likely
- Probability: interpreting outcomes of games
- Probability: making predictions that are based on data (for example, telling if an event is most likely or least likely)
- Problem solving: drawing a picture, finding a pattern, working backward, making a list, estimating, or using logic

Name _____

Pancakes Aplenty

Use the code to color the
pancakes.
Answer the questions below.
Use the graph.

Color Code:
Color the pancake **brown.**
Color the butter **yellow.**
Color the syrup **red.**

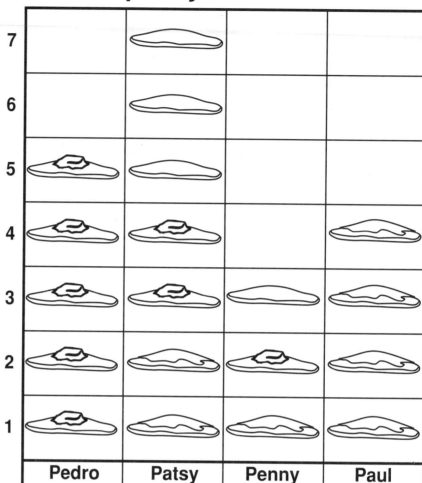

1. Who ate the most pancakes? _____

2. Who ate the fewest pancakes? _____

3. Who ate the most pancakes with butter? _____

4. Who ate the fewest pancakes with butter? _____

5. Who ate the most pancakes with syrup? _____

6. Who ate the fewest pancakes with syrup? _____

7. How many pancakes did Pedro and Penny eat altogether? _____

8. How many pancakes did Patsy and Paul eat altogether? _____

9. How many more pancakes did Pedro eat than Paul? _____

10. Who ate one more pancake than Penny? _____

11. Who ate two more pancakes than Pedro? _____

12. How many more pancakes did Patsy eat than Penny? _____

Champion Chewers

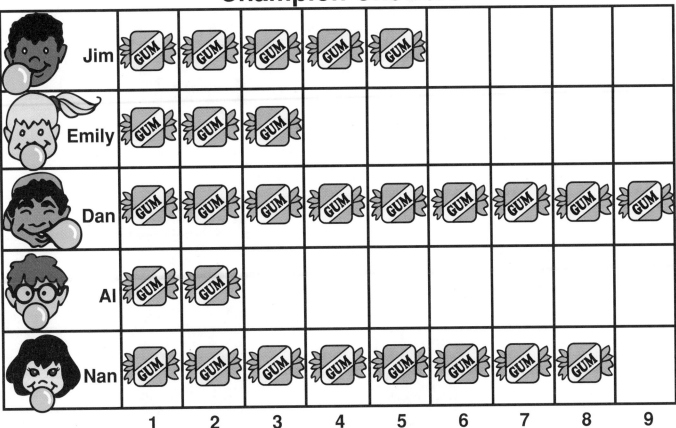

		1	2	3	4	5	6	7	8	9

Read the graph. Answer the questions.

1. Who chewed the most pieces of gum? _____

2. Who chewed the fewest pieces of gum? _____

3. How many pieces did Jim and Al chew altogether? _____

4. How many pieces did Emily, Al, and Nan chew altogether? _____

5. How many more pieces did Dan chew than Nan? _____

6. How many more pieces did Jim chew than Emily? _____

7. How many fewer pieces did Emily chew than Nan? _____

8. How many fewer pieces did Jim chew than Dan? _____

9. Who chewed 5 pieces of gum? _____

10. Who chewed 8 pieces of gum? _____

At Home: Look no further than your kitchen cabinet for sources of pictograph material. Ask your child to make a graph showing how many boxes of cereal, how many cans, and how many packages of chips or cookies are on the shelves. Assist her in drawing a three-row graph on a sheet of paper. Next, help her determine a symbol, such as a rectangle for a cereal box, to represent each category. Then have her record the information on her graph. When she's through, ask her to describe the information on the complete graph.

Name _____

Soup du Jour!

Chef Pierre was very busy during lunch today!
This graph shows the soup he sold.
Use the graph to answer the questions below.

	vegetable	tomato	chicken noodle	wild rice	French onion
10					
9	▓				
8	▓			▓	
7	▓			▓	▓
6	▓			▓	▓
5	▓	▓		▓	▓
4	▓	▓		▓	▓
3	▓	▓	▓	▓	▓
2	▓	▓	▓	▓	▓
1	▓	▓	▓	▓	▓

Number of Bowls

Types of Soup

1. What soup was sold the most?_____ The least? _____

2. Were more bowls of tomato and chicken noodle soup sold or French onion soup?

   _____

3. How many more bowls of wild rice soup were sold than tomato soup? _____

4. How many more bowls of chicken noodle soup need to be sold to equal the

   amount of vegetable soup sold? _____

5. How many bowls of soup did Chef Pierre sell? _____

Try This: Vegetable soup costs $.10 a bowl. Chicken noodle soup costs $.25 a bowl. How much more money did Chef Pierre make selling vegetable soup?

Sizing Up Dinosaurs

Graph the length of each dinosaur listed on the graph.

Stegosaurus   = 25 feet
Euoplocephalus = 20 feet
Tryannosaurus   = 40 feet
Allosaurus   = 30 feet
Coelophysis   = 10 feet
Triceratops   = 30 feet
Brachiosaurus   = 75 feet

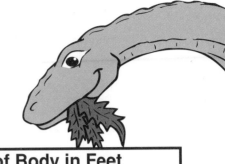

Type of Dinosaur	Length of Body in Feet						
	10	20	30	40	50	60	70
Stegosaurus							
Euoplocephalus							
Tyrannosaurus							
Allosaurus							
Coelophysis							
Triceratops							
Brachiosaurus							

Now use the bar graph to answer each question.

1. Which two dinosaurs were the same length?

_____
_____

2. Which dinosaur was the shortest?

_____

3. Which dinosaur was the longest?

_____

4. How much longer was Tyrannosaurus than Triceratops?

_____

5. How much shorter was Coelophysis than Allosaurus?

_____

6. Which dinosaur was longer than Coelophysis and shorter than Stegosaurus?

_____

Name _____

Heads or Tails?

1. PREDICT how many heads and tails you will get if you flip a coin 20 times.

Heads _____   Tails _____

2. FLIP a coin 20 times.
   For each coin flip, COLOR one box.

Heads

Tails

3. COUNT and RECORD the data you collected.

Heads _____   Tails _____

4. COMPARE your data with your parent's data.
   DESCRIBE what you discover.

_____

_____

_____

5. THINK about what you have learned.
   PREDICT how many heads and tails you will get if you flip the coin 40 times.

   Heads _____   Tails _____

   EXPLAIN why you made this prediction.

   _____

   _____

   _____

At Home: Place five red checkers and one black one in a bag. Ask your child to predict which color will be chosen if one is randomly removed from the bag. Have her remove one and record its color before replacing it in the bag. Have her repeat this ten more times; then ask her to look at the results. For a challenge, ask her to fill the bag so there is a greater probability of choosing a black checker.

What's the Chance?

1. LOOK inside your paper bag.
   WRITE the color of each marble on a line.
   In each circle PREDICT how many times you
   will grab each color of marble if you reach
   inside the bag 20 times.

   _____   _____

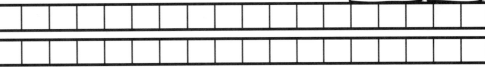

2. WRITE the marble colors on the lines.
   REACH inside the bag 20 times and GRAB one marble each time.
   For each marble you grab, COLOR one box.

   _____

   _____

3. COUNT and RECORD the data you collected
   in the box at the right.

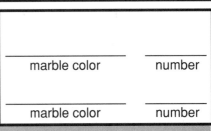

   _____   _____
   marble color   number

   _____   _____
   marble color   number

4. COMPARE your data with your parent's data.
   DESCRIBE what you discover.

   _____

   _____

5. THINK about what you have learned.
   PREDICT what will happen if you repeat
   the activity using three different
   marbles.

   _____

   _____

   EXPLAIN your prediction.

   _____

At Home: To prepare for this activity, provide your child with a paper bag containing two different colors of marbles. He will also need crayons and a pencil.

Let's Go for a Spin!

Read each problem.
Look at each spinner.
Circle the spinners you would use.
Underline a spinner if you are certain it would get the spin.

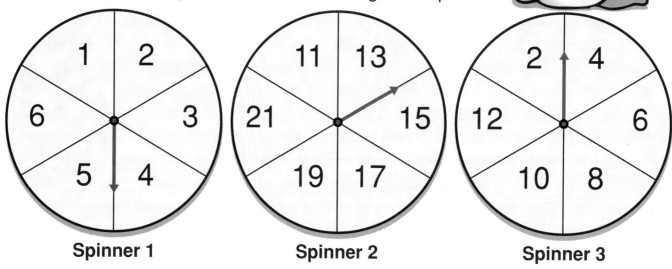

Spinner 1　　　　**Spinner 2**　　　　**Spinner 3**

1. If you want to spin a 2, you could use: Spinner 1　　Spinner 2　　Spinner 3	4. If you want to spin a number larger than 8, you could use: Spinner 1　　Spinner 2　　Spinner 3
2. If you want to spin an even number, you could use: Spinner 1　　Spinner 2　　Spinner 3	5. If you want to spin an odd number, you could use: Spinner 1　　Spinner 2　　Spinner 3
3. If you want to spin a 2-digit number, you could use: Spinner 1　　Spinner 2　　Spinner 3	6. If you want to spin a number less than 10, you could use: Spinner 1　　Spinner 2　　Spinner 3

Here's to Chance!

Color the squares so that all the same numbers are the same color.
Then answer the questions.

1	4	2	3	2	5	4
5	5	5	5	2	5	5
2	5	3	1	3	4	5
2	2	4	5	2	5	3

Bill and Joe play a game.
Each one drops a penny on the gameboard.
They each do this 10 times.

1. What is the number the penny is **most** likely to land on? _____

2. What is the number the penny is **least** likely to land on? _____

3. The two numbers that have equal chances of being landed on are _____ and _____.

4. Is there a better chance of landing on a 1 or a 3? _____

5. Is there a better chance of landing on a 2 or a 4? _____

Try This: Play the game with a partner. Keep a tally to show how many times you land on each number.

Name_____

Lots of Legs!

Read each problem.
Draw and color a picture of the problem in the large box.
Circle the correct answer in the small box.

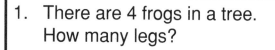

1. There are 4 frogs in a tree. How many legs?

| 12 | 16 | 18 |

2. There are 3 elephants eating plants. How many legs?

| 8 | 12 | 15 |

3. There are 5 ostriches and 2 butterflies. Which group has more legs?

| the ostrich group | the butterfly group |

4. A cheetah runs by, chasing an ostrich. How many legs?

| 2 | 4 | 6 |

5. There are 2 ants and 3 penguins. Which group has fewer legs?

| the ant group | the penguin group |

6. How many frogs are needed to have the same number of legs as 2 ants?

| 3 | 4 | 5 |

Name _____

The Hug-a-Cub Cookout

Saturday is the camp cookout.
Happy Trails Cabin must complete its food order.

There are 8 bear cubs in Happy Trails Cabin.
Finish each chart to find out how much food to order.

Each cub will eat 2 hot dogs.

Number of bear cubs	0	1	2	3	4	5	6	7	8
Number of hot dogs	0	2	4	6					

Each cub will eat 5 pickles.

Number of bear cubs	0	1	2	3	4	5	6	7	8
Number of pickles	0	5	10	15					

Each cub will eat 8 potato chips.

Number of bear cubs	0	1	2	3	4	5	6	7	8
Number of potato chips	0	8	16						

Potato Chips
Cub Size

Each cub will eat 4 cookies.

Number of bear cubs	0	1	2	3	4	5	6	7	8
Number of cookies	0	4	8						

Each cub will eat 3 marshmallows.

Number of bear cubs	0	1	2	3	4	5	6	7	8
Number of marshmallows	0	3	6						

Bear-in-Mind Marshmallows

Use the completed charts to fill out the food order form.

Camp Cookout Food Order

Cabin: _____

Number of each:
_____ hot dogs   _____ potato chips
_____ pickles   _____ cookies   _____ marshmallows

Name _____

Name That Student!

Read each clue.
Find the matching dinosaur.
Write its name on the desk.

| _____ | _____ | _____ |
| Dinosaur | Dinosaur | Dinosaur |

1. Drew Dinosaur does not have plates.
2. Dee Dinosaur sits beside a dinosaur with a long neck.
3. Don Dinosaur sits between Drew and Dee.

Cut out each box.
Read the clues.
Glue each set of clues below the matching dinosaur.

This dinosaur wears four shoes at recess.
His name is Larry Longneck.

Rep Dial has sharp claws.
She shines her plates every day before school.

Dino Might's big tail helps him balance when he walks to school.
He uses his sharp teeth to eat a school lunch.

Answer Keys

Page 6

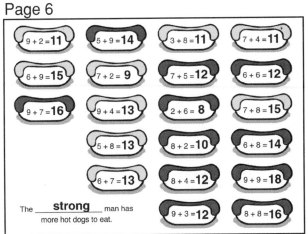

9 + 2 = **11**	5 + 9 = **14**	3 + 8 = **11**	7 + 4 = **11**
6 + 9 = **15**	7 + 2 = **9**	7 + 5 = **12**	6 + 6 = **12**
9 + 7 = **16**	9 + 4 = **13**	2 + 6 = **8**	7 + 8 = **15**
	5 + 8 = **13**	8 + 2 = **10**	6 + 8 = **14**
	6 + 7 = **13**	8 + 4 = **12**	9 + 9 = **18**
		9 + 3 = **12**	8 + 8 = **16**

The ___**strong**___ man has more hot dogs to eat.

Page 7

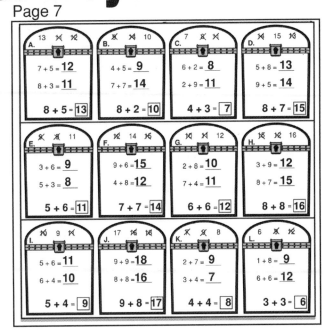

A. 13
7 + 5 = **12**
8 + 3 = **11**
8 + 5 = **13**

B. 10
4 + 5 = **9**
7 + 7 = **14**
8 + 2 = **10**

C. 7
6 + 2 = **8**
2 + 9 = **11**
4 + 3 = **7**

D. 15
5 + 8 = **13**
9 + 5 = **14**
8 + 7 = **15**

E. 11
3 + 6 = **9**
5 + 3 = **8**
5 + 6 = **11**

F. 14
9 + 6 = **15**
4 + 8 = **12**
7 + 7 = **14**

G. 12
2 + 8 = **10**
7 + 4 = **11**
6 + 6 = **12**

H. 16
3 + 9 = **12**
8 + 7 = **15**
8 + 8 = **16**

I. 9
5 + 6 = **11**
6 + 4 = **10**
5 + 4 = **9**

J. 17
9 + 9 = **18**
8 + 8 = **16**
9 + 8 = **17**

K. 8
2 + 7 = **9**
3 + 4 = **7**
4 + 4 = **8**

L. 6
1 + 8 = **9**
6 + 6 = **12**
3 + 3 = **6**

Page 8

8 + 2 = **10**   3 + 5 = **8**
6 + 5 = **11**   5 + 9 = **14**   5 + 7 = **12**
6 + 6 = **12**   4 + 9 = **13**   8 + 9 = **17**

1st Place
5 + 8 = **13**   9 + 7 = **16**
7 + 7 = **14**   8 + 6 = **14**   7 + 8 = **15**
9 + 9 = **18**   9 + 6 = **15**   6 + 7 = **13**

6 + 9 = **15**   8 + 7 = **15**
9 + 8 = **17**   6 + 4 = **10**   9 + 5 = **14**
5 + 5 = **10**   10 + 7 = **17**   8 + 8 = **16**

9 + 2 = **11**   7 + 4 = **11**
8 + 5 = **13**   10 + 6 = **16**   6 + 3 = **9**
4 + 8 = **12**   6 + 8 = **14**   7 + 9 = **16**

Page 9

1.	5 6 +9 **20**	2.	7 8 +2 **17**	3.	6 6 +2 **14**	4.	3 6 +7 **16**	5.	6 9 +9 **24**	6.	8 1 +9 **18**	7.	7 9 +3 **19**

8.	2 3 +8 **13**	9.	5 6 +3 **14**	10.	7 3 +7 **17**	11.	2 6 +5 **13**	12.	3 7 +2 **12**	13.	6 5 +4 **15**	14.	6 7 +3 **16**

15.	4 7 +5 **16**	16.	9 1 +2 **12**	17.	5 4 +4 **13**	18.	6 5 +6 **17**	19.	2 9 +3 **14**	20.	7 9 +4 **20**	21.	6 3 +5 **14**

Try This: If each Martian has three eyes, how many eyes will three Martians have? Draw a picture that shows your answer. **9**

Page 10

5 +8 **13**	2 +9 **11**	7 +7 **14**	8 +6 **14**	1 +4 **5**

7 + 5 = **12**   4 + 4 = **8**   9 + 4 = **13**
5 + 6 = **11**   8 + 8 = **16**   5 + 9 = **14**
8 + 9 = **17**   7 + 7 = **14**   7 + 9 = **16**
6 + 7 = **13**   9 + 9 = **18**   6 + 3 = **9**
2 + 5 = **7**   4 + 7 = **11**   8 + 3 = **11**

Try This: Draw an orange circle around each sum that is greater than 10. You should have 18 circles.

7 +8 **15**	4 +5 **9**	8 +2 **10**	9 +6 **15**	3 +7 **10**

18 − 9 = **9**
14 − 9 = **5**
13 − 6 = **7**
13 − 5 = **8**
12 − 9 = **3**
11 − 4 = **7**
14 − 6 = **8**

16 −8 **8**	15 −9 **6**	10 −6 **4**	16 −9 **7**	14 −5 **9**	11 −7 **4**

17 −8 **9**	11 −2 **9**	16 −7 **9**	12 −7 **5**	13 −8 **5**

13 − 4 = **9**   15 − 7 = **8**
12 − 5 = **7**   13 − 7 = **6**

Try This: If you have six facts that equal nine, color the lion's nose pink.

Page 11

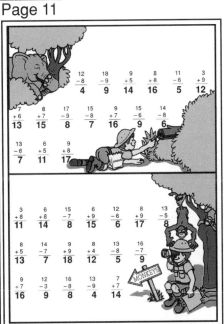

12 −8 **4**	18 −9 **9**	9 +5 **14**	8 +8 **16**	11 −6 **5**	3 +9 **12**

7 +6 **13**	8 +7 **15**	17 −9 **8**	15 −8 **7**	9 +7 **16**	15 −6 **9**	14 −8 **6**

13 −6 **7**	6 +5 **11**	9 +8 **17**

3 +8 **11**	6 +8 **14**	15 −7 **8**	6 +9 **15**	12 −6 **6**	8 +9 **17**	13 −5 **8**

8 +5 **13**	14 −7 **7**	9 +9 **18**	8 +4 **12**	13 −8 **5**	16 −7 **9**

9 +7 **16**	12 −3 **9**	16 −8 **8**	13 −9 **4**	7 +7 **14**

Page 12

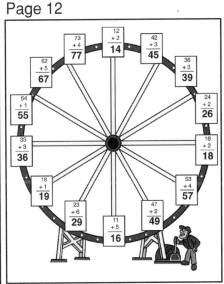

73 +4 **77**	12 +2 **14**	42 +3 **45**

62 +5 **67**		36 +3 **39**

54 +1 **55**		24 +2 **26**

33 +3 **36**		16 +2 **18**

18 +1 **19**		53 +4 **57**

23 +6 **29**	11 +5 **16**	47 +2 **49**

123

Page 13

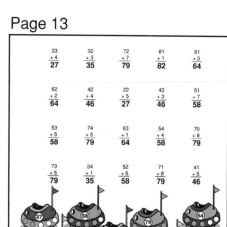

23 + 4 **27**	32 + 3 **35**	72 + 7 **79**	81 + 1 **82**	61 + 3 **64**
62 + 2 **64**	42 + 4 **46**	22 + 5 **27**	43 + 3 **46**	51 + 7 **58**
53 + 5 **58**	74 + 5 **79**	63 + 1 **64**	54 + 4 **58**	70 + 9 **79**
73 + 6 **79**	34 + 1 **35**	52 + 6 **58**	71 + 8 **79**	41 + 5 **46**

27 58 79 64 35 82 46

Which car got the least bumps? **82**
Which car got the most bumps? **79**

Page 14

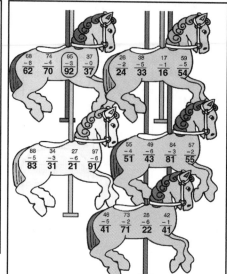

68 − 6 **62**	74 − 4 **70**	95 − 3 **92**	37 − 0 **37**	26 − 2 **24**	38 − 5 **33**	17 − 1 **16**	59 − 5 **54**

88 − 5 **83**	34 − 3 **31**	27 − 6 **21**	97 − 6 **91**	55 − 4 **51**	49 − 6 **43**	84 − 3 **81**	57 − 2 **55**

46 − 5 **41**	73 − 2 **71**	28 − 6 **22**	42 − 1 **41**

Page 15

1. 15
2. 25
3. 19
4. 35
5. 49
6. 10
7. 21
8. 46
9. 12
10. 20

Page 16

A. How many tens? **2** / How many ones? **3** / 12 + 11 = **23**	B. How many tens? **1** / How many ones? **8** / 11 + 7 = **18**
C. How many tens? **2** / How many ones? **9** / 13 + 16 = **29**	D. How many tens? **1** / How many ones? **6** / 12 + 4 = **16**
E. How many tens? **2** / How many ones? **8** / 14 + 14 = **28**	F. How many tens? **2** / How many ones? **8** / 16 + 12 = **28**
G. How many tens? **2** / How many ones? **8** / 15 + 13 = **28**	H. How many tens? **1** / How many ones? **9** / 11 + 8 = **19**

Page 18

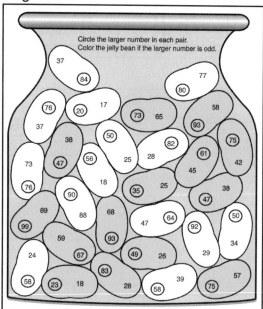

Circle the larger number in each pair.
Color the jelly bean if the larger number is odd.

Page 19

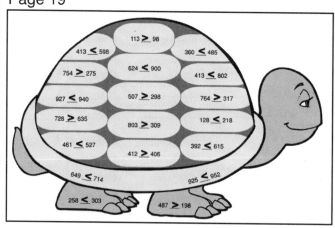

113 > 98
413 < 598   360 < 485
754 > 275   624 < 900   413 < 802
927 < 940   507 > 298   764 > 317
728 > 635   803 > 309   128 < 218
461 < 527   392 < 615
412 > 406
649 < 714   925 < 952
258 < 303   487 > 198

Page 20

1. 95
2. 17
3. 59
4. 71, 83
5. 26 < 32,
62 > 45
6. 40 > 34
7. 10
8. 10 < 78

Page 21

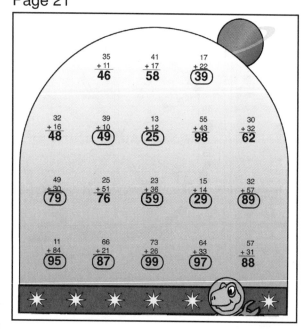

35 + 11 **46**	41 + 17 **58**	17 + 22 **(39)**		
32 + 16 **48**	39 + 10 **(49)**	13 + 12 **(25)**	55 + 43 **98**	30 + 32 **62**
49 + 30 **(79)**	25 + 51 **76**	23 + 36 **(59)**	15 + 14 **(29)**	32 + 57 **(89)**
11 + 84 **(95)**	66 + 21 **(87)**	73 + 26 **(99)**	64 + 33 **(97)**	57 + 31 **88**

Page 22

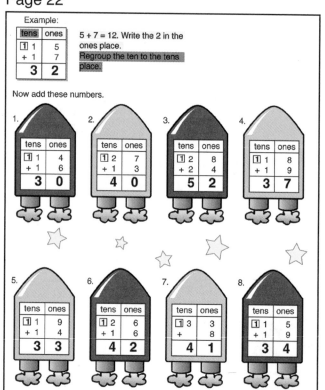

Example:

tens	ones
[1] 1	5
+ 1	7
3	**2**

5 + 7 = 12. Write the 2 in the ones place.
Regroup the ten to the tens place.

Now add these numbers.

1.
tens	ones
[1] 1	4
+ 1	6
3	**0**

2.
tens	ones
[1] 2	7
+ 1	3
4	**0**

3.
tens	ones
[1] 2	8
+ 2	4
5	**2**

4.
tens	ones
[1] 1	8
+ 1	9
3	**7**

5.
tens	ones
[1] 1	9
+ 1	4
3	**3**

6.
tens	ones
[1] 2	6
+ 1	6
4	**2**

7.
tens	ones
[1] 3	3
+	8
4	**1**

8.
tens	ones
[1] 1	5
+ 1	9
3	**4**

Page 23

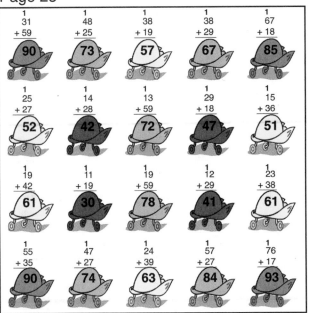

31 + 59 = **90**	48 + 25 = **73**	38 + 19 = **57**	38 + 29 = **67**	67 + 18 = **85**
25 + 27 = **52**	14 + 28 = **42**	13 + 59 = **72**	29 + 18 = **47**	15 + 36 = **51**
19 + 42 = **61**	11 + 19 = **30**	19 + 59 = **78**	12 + 29 = **41**	23 + 38 = **61**
55 + 35 = **90**	47 + 27 = **74**	24 + 39 = **63**	57 + 27 = **84**	76 + 17 = **93**

Page 24

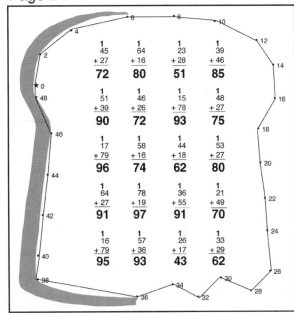

45 + 27 = **72**	64 + 16 = **80**	23 + 28 = **51**	39 + 46 = **85**
51 + 39 = **90**	46 + 26 = **72**	15 + 78 = **93**	48 + 27 = **75**
17 + 79 = **96**	58 + 16 = **74**	44 + 18 = **62**	53 + 27 = **80**
64 + 27 = **91**	78 + 19 = **97**	36 + 55 = **91**	21 + 49 = **70**
16 + 79 = **95**	57 + 36 = **93**	26 + 17 = **43**	33 + 29 = **62**

Page 25

36¢ + 45¢ = 81¢ = D	57¢ + 28¢ = 85¢ = P	15¢ + 26¢ = 41¢ = A	72¢ + 19¢ = 91¢ = M	48¢ + 39¢ = 87¢ = N	54¢ + 18¢ = 72¢ = T
54¢ + 38¢ = 92¢ = E	25¢ + 17¢ = 42¢ = R	16¢ + 77¢ = 93¢ = U	37¢ + 47¢ = 84¢ = B	56¢ + 18¢ = 74¢ = U	49¢ + 49¢ = 98¢ = U
39¢ + 11¢ = 50¢ = T	76¢ + 14¢ = 90¢ = U	51¢ + 19¢ = 70¢ = A	22¢ + 29¢ = 51¢ = T	13¢ + 18¢ = 31¢ = S	31¢ + 29¢ = 60¢ = S

P e a n u t   B u t t e r and
85¢ 60¢ 70¢ 87¢ 90¢ 72¢   84¢ 93¢ 51¢ 74¢ 92¢ 42¢

M u s t a r d
91¢ 98¢ 31¢ 50¢ 41¢ 42¢ 81¢

Page 26

16 + 15 = **31** = E	26 + 27 = **53** = H	
17 + 24 = **41** = E	49 + 23 = **72** = N	57 + 37 = **94** = S
26 + 19 = **45** = L	36 + 54 = **90** = A	19 + 45 = **64** = B
38 + 23 = **61** = E	55 + 15 = **70** = I	37 + 38 = **75** = E
37 + 45 = **82** = D	49 + 19 = **68** = U	45 + 46 = **91** = Y
68 + 15 = **83** = A	48 + 38 = **86** = E	37 + 19 = **57** = F
17 + 59 = **76** = C	57 + 23 = **80** = C	29 + 48 = **77** = E

To solve the riddle, match the letters to the numbered lines below.

B e c a u s e   h e
64 41 80 83 66 94 86   53 75

n e e d e d   a   l i f t!
72 61 31 57 77 82   90   45 70 76 91

Page 27

Example:
a. 84 − 25 = 59, 59 + 25 = 84
b. 89 − 29 = 60, 60 + 29 = 89
c. 72 − 34 = 38, 38 + 34 = 72
d. 53 − 17 = 36, 36 + 17 = 53
e. 79 − 54 = 25, 25 + 54 = 79
f. 63 − 29 = 34, 34 + 29 = 63
g. 76 − 32 = 44, 44 + 32 = 76
h. 86 − 47 = 39, 39 + 47 = 86
i. 74 − 46 = 28, 28 + 26 = 54
j. 62 − 19 = 43, 43 + 19 = 62
k. 96 − 55 = 41, 41 + 55 = 96
l. 26 − 18 = 8, 8 + 18 = 26
m. 43 − 28 = 15, 15 + 28 = 43
n. 85 − 43 = 42, 42 + 43 = 85
o. 85 − 64 = 21, 21 + 64 = 85
p. 79 − 36 = 43, 43 + 36 = 79

Page 28

1. 48 + 23 = **71** (L)	2. 50 − 25 = **25** (A)	3. 71 − 35 = **36** (A)	4. 19 + 11 = **30** (S)
5. 87 − 18 = **79** (D)	6. 27 + 18 = **45** (G)	7. 80 − 52 = **28** (L)	8. 91 − 73 = **18** (R)
9. 57 − 28 = **29** (H)	10. 31 + 29 = **60** (E)	11. 63 − 24 = **39** (E)	12. 38 + 16 = **54** (N)
13. 39 + 55 = **94** (I)	14. 19 + 31 = **50** (N)	15. 59 + 11 = **70** (D)	16. 82 − 46 = **16** (D)

Write the letter that matches each answer to discover the answer to the riddle.

Answer:
H A N S E L   A N D   "G R I D D L E"
29 36 54 30 39 71 25 50 16   45 18 94 79 70 28 60

Page 29

1. 19 balloons
2. 11 sandwiches
3. 14 penguins
4. 17 prizes
5. 6 pictures
6. 18 songs
7. 14 to sit on
8. 16 hats

Page 30

1. 39
2. 75¢
3. 31
4. 28
5. 27
6. 8
7. 52
8. 50¢
9. 24
10. 46¢

Page 31

1. 8
2. 6
3. 1
4. 7
5. 5
6. 8
7. 7
8. 3

Page 32

1. 55
2. 44
3. 32
4. 47
5. 64
6. 23

Page 34

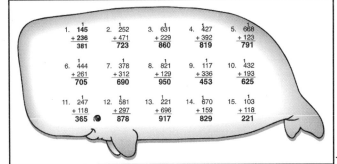

1. 145 + 236 = **381**	2. 252 + 471 = **723**	3. 631 + 229 = **860**	4. 427 + 392 = **819**	5. 668 + 123 = **791**
6. 444 + 261 = **705**	7. 378 + 312 = **690**	8. 821 + 129 = **950**	9. 117 + 336 = **453**	10. 432 + 193 = **625**
11. 247 + 118 = **365**	12. 581 + 297 = **878**	13. 221 + 696 = **917**	14. 670 + 159 = **829**	15. 103 + 118 = **221**

Page 35

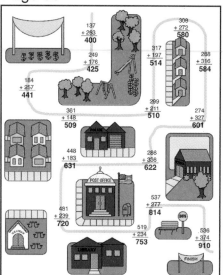

137 + 263 = 400
308 + 272 = 580
249 + 176 = 425
317 + 197 = 514
266 + 316 = 584
184 + 257 = 441
361 + 148 = 509
299 + 211 = 510
274 + 327 = 601
448 + 183 = 631
266 + 356 = 622
537 + 277 = 814
481 + 239 = 720
519 + 234 = 753
536 + 374 = 910

Page 42

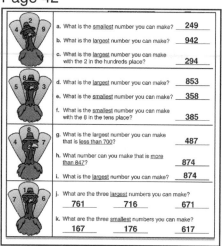

a. What is the smallest number you can make? **249**
b. What is the largest number you can make? **942**
c. What is the largest number you can make with the 2 in the hundreds place? **294**
d. What is the largest number you can make? **853**
e. What is the smallest number you can make? **358**
f. What is the smallest number you can make with the 8 in the tens place? **385**
g. What is the largest number you can make that is less than 700? **487**
h. What number can you make that is more than 847? **874**
i. What is the largest number you can make? **874**
j. What are the three largest numbers you can make? **761 716 671**
k. What are the three smallest numbers you can make? **167 176 617**

Page 43

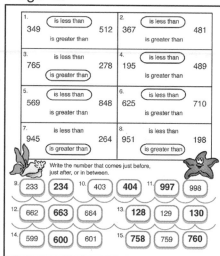

1. 349 — is less than — 512 — is greater than	2. 367 — is less than — 481 — is greater than
3. 765 — is less than — 278 — is greater than	4. 195 — is less than — 489 — is greater than
5. 569 — is less than — 848 — is greater than	6. 625 — is less than — 710 — is greater than
7. 945 — is less than — 264 — is greater than	8. 951 — is less than — 198 — is greater than

Write the number that comes just before, just after, or in between.

9. 233 **234**   10. 403 **404**   11. **997** 998
12. 662 **663** 664   13. **128** 129 **130**
14. 599 **600** 601   15. **758** 759 **760**

Page 44

tens	ones
2	14
(1)	4
−1	6
1	**8**

tens	ones
3	13
(2)	3
−2	9
1	**4**

tens	ones
5	15
(4)	5
−3	7
2	**8**

tens	ones
4	11
(3)	1
−1	8
3	**3**

tens	ones
6	13
(5)	3
−2	9
4	**4**

tens	ones
7	12
(6)	2
−1	7
6	**5**

tens	ones
8	10
(7)	0
−3	4
5	**6**

tens	ones
1	18
(0)	8
−	9
1	**9**

tens	ones
2	16
(1)	6
−1	9
1	**7**

tens	ones
4	14
(3)	4
−2	5
2	**9**

tens	ones
5	13
(4)	3
−2	6
3	**7**

tens	ones
6	17
(5)	7
−1	8
5	**9**

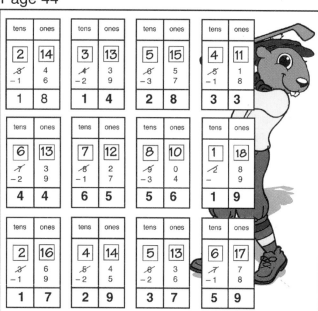

Page 45

1.
hundreds	tens	ones
4	10	
(3)	(9)	6
−3	8	2
1	2	4

2.
hundreds	tens	ones
6	13	
(5)	(8)	8
−4	5	2
2	**8**	**6**

3.
hundreds	tens	ones
	7	11
3	(6)	1
−1	7	4
2	**0**	**7**

4.
hundreds	tens	ones
6	4	5
−2	0	3
4	**4**	**2**

5.
hundreds	tens	ones
2	14	
(1)	(3)	5 0
−2	7	
	7	**5**

6.
hundreds	tens	ones
7	17	
(6)	(6)	4 3
−2	8	
5	**9**	**1**

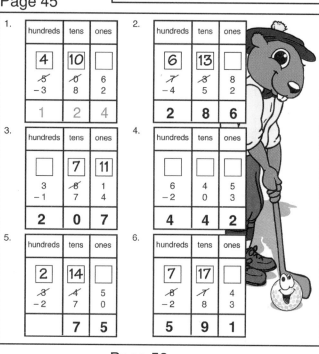

Page 47

1. **Birdie Bubba:** Putter Pizza / Caddy Cola — $3.78 + 1.06 = $4.84
2. **Eagle Ed:** Nine-Iron Nachos / Sand-Trap Shake — $1.44 + 2.47 = $3.91
3. **Bogey Bob:** Tee-Time Taco / Fairway Fries — $1.88 + 1.62 = $3.50
4. **Drivin' Diane:** Double-Bogey Burger / Sand-Trap Shake — $3.39 + 2.47 = $5.86
5. **Flyin' Fran:** Hole-in-One Hot Dog / Caddy Cola — $2.25 + 1.06 = $3.31
6. **Teein' Tom:** Fairway Fries / Sand-Trap Shake — $1.62 + 2.47 = $4.09
7. **Hole-in-One Hank:** Putter Pizza / Sand-Trap Shake — $3.78 + 2.47 = $6.25
8. **Putterin' Patty:** Tee-Time Taco / Nine-Iron Nachos — $1.88 + 1.44 = $3.32
9. **Outta' There Otto:** Hole-in-One Hot Dog / Sand-Trap Shake — $2.25 + 2.47 = $4.72
10. **Up-To-Par Paul:** Double-Bogey Burger / Fairway Fries — $3.39 + 1.62 = $5.01
11. **Nine-Iron Ned:** Tee-Time Taco / Caddy Cola — $1.88 + 1.06 = $2.94
12. **Sand-Trap Sue:** Putter Pizza / Hole-in-One Hot Dog — $3.78 + 2.25 = $6.03

Page 48

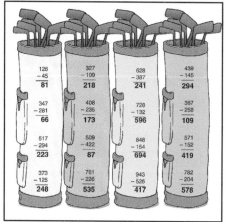

126 − 45 = 81
327 − 109 = 218
628 − 387 = 241
439 − 145 = 294
347 − 281 = 66
408 − 235 = 173
728 − 132 = 596
367 − 258 = 109
517 − 294 = 223
509 − 422 = 87
848 − 154 = 694
571 − 152 = 419
373 − 125 = 248
761 − 226 = 535
943 − 526 = 417
782 − 204 = 578

Page 49

1. 2   3. 4   5. 7   7. 4
2. 3   4. 6   6. 5   8. 2

Page 52

5 ×4 = **20**	3 ×2 = **6**	2 ×2 = **4**	2 ×9 = **18**	8 ×1 = **8**
4 ×7 = **28**	5 ×2 = **10**	3 ×5 = **15**	4 ×8 = **32**	2 ×6 = **12**
2 ×3 = **6**	4 ×2 = **8**	3 ×4 = **12**	2 ×5 = **10**	4 ×1 = **4**
5 ×1 = **5**	2 ×8 = **16**	5 ×3 = **15**	3 ×3 = **9**	5 ×6 = **30**	3 ×9 = **27**
3 ×8 = **24**	5 ×5 = **25**	4 ×9 = **36**	2 ×4 = **8**	5 ×8 = **40**	5 ×9 = **45**
5 ×7 = **35**	4 ×6 = **24**	9 ×1 = **9**	4 ×0 = **0**	4 ×3 = **12**	

2 x 7 = **14**   6 x 3 = **18**   4 x 4 = **16**

4 x 5 = **20**   5 x 0 = **0**   3 x 7 = **21**

Page 53

Game Winners
Game A   **O**
Game B   **X**
Game C   **O**
Game D   **X**

Page 54

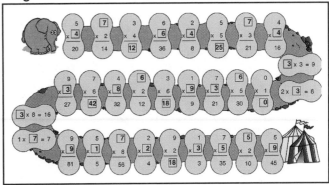

Page 64

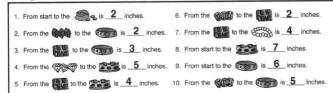

Ship's Log		
Places Traveled	**Distance In Inches**	**Distance In Miles**
Sunken Skull Island to Pirate's Lookout	2	4
Pirate's Lookout to Canary Perch Isle	3	6
Canary Perch Isle to Crosspoint Island	2	4
Crosspoint Island to Jewel Isle	2	4
Jewel Isle to Danger Island	4	8
Danger Island to Crosspoint Island	4	8
Crosspoint Island to Quicksand Point	1	2
Quicksand Point to Jewel Isle	2	4

Page 65

1. From start to the 🐾 is **2** inches.
2. From the 💎 to the 👑 is **2** inches.
3. From the 🏰 to the 💍 is **3** inches.
4. From the 💎 to the 🏺 is **5** inches.
5. From the 🏰 to the 🏺 is **4** inches.
6. From the 👑 to the 🏰 is **2** inches.
7. From the 🏰 to the 🦷 is **4** inches.
8. From start to the 💎 is **7** inches.
9. From start to the 💍 is **6** inches.
10. From the 👑 to the 💍 is **5** inches.

Page 75

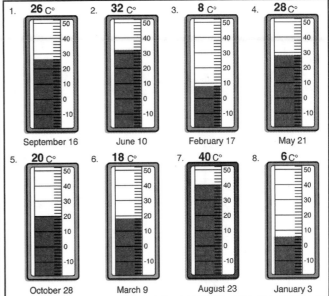

1. **26** C° — September 16
2. **32** C° — June 10
3. **8** C° — February 17
4. **28** C° — May 21
5. **20** C° — October 28
6. **18** C° — March 9
7. **40** C° — August 23
8. **6** C° — January 3

Page 76

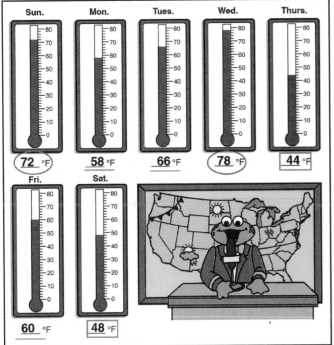

Sun.	Mon.	Tues.	Wed.	Thurs.
72 °F	**58** °F	**66** °F	**78** °F	**44** °F

Fri.	Sat.
60 °F	**48** °F

Page 85

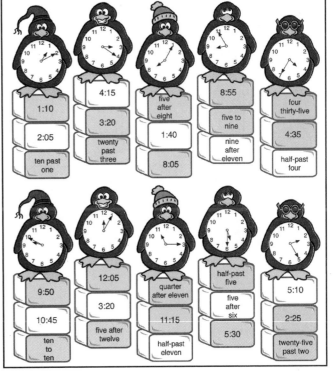

1:10 — 2:05 — ten past one
4:15 — 3:20 — twenty past three
five after eight — 1:40 — 8:05
8:55 — five to nine — nine after eleven
four thirty-five — 4:35 — half-past four

9:50 — 10:45 — ten to ten
12:05 — 3:20 — five after twelve
quarter after eleven — 11:15 — half-past eleven
half-past five — five after six — 5:30
5:10 — 2:25 — twenty-five past two

Page 88

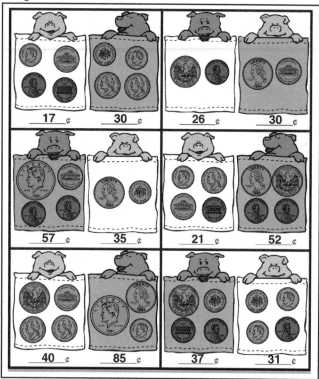

17 ¢	30 ¢	26 ¢	30 ¢
57 ¢	35 ¢	21 ¢	52 ¢
40 ¢	85 ¢	37 ¢	31 ¢

Page 89

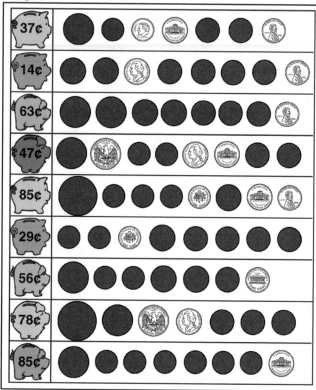

Page 91

Amount	quarters	dimes	nickels	pennies
35¢	1	1	0	0
24¢	0	2	0	4
40¢	1	1	1	0
60¢	2	1	0	0
51¢	2	0	0	1
32¢	1	0	1	2
15¢	0	1	1	0
25¢	1	0	0	0
70¢	2	2	0	0
38¢	1	1	0	3
20¢	0	2	0	0
14¢	0	1	0	4
47¢	1	2	0	2

Page 102

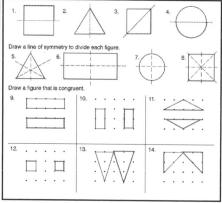

Draw a line of symmetry to divide each figure.

Draw a figure that is congruent.

Page 107

1. 16 triangles
2. 5 squares
3. 10 circles
4. 2 rectangles
5. 15 triangles
6. 24 circles and rectangles

Page 104

1. How many squares are in this rectangle? __6__

2. How many squares are in this triangle? __5__
   How many triangles? __11__
   How many rectangles? __4__

3. Draw a shape that is congruent.
   Then draw a line of symmetry.

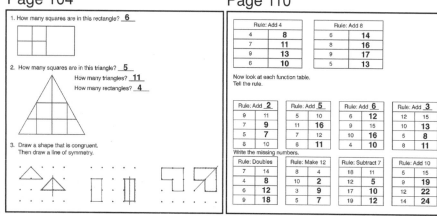

Page 103

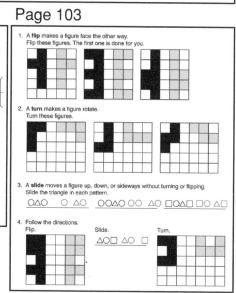

1. A **flip** makes a figure face the other way.
   Flip these figures. The first one is done for you.

2. A **turn** makes a figure rotate.
   Turn these figures.

3. A **slide** moves a figure up, down, or sideways without turning or flipping.
   Slide the triangle in each pattern.

4. Follow the directions.
   Flip.   Slide.   Turn.

Page 110

Rule: Add 4	
4	**8**
7	**11**
9	**13**
6	**10**

Rule: Add 8	
6	**14**
8	**16**
9	**17**
5	**13**

Now look at each function table.
Tell the rule.

Rule: Add **2**	
9	11
7	**9**
5	7
8	10

Rule: Add **5**	
5	10
11	**16**
7	12
6	**11**

Rule: Add **6**	
6	**12**
9	15
10	**16**
4	**10**

Rule: Add **3**	
12	15
10	**13**
5	**8**
8	**11**

Write the missing numbers.

Rule: Doubles	
7	14
4	**8**
6	**12**
9	**18**

Rule: Make 12	
8	4
10	**2**
3	**9**
5	**7**

Rule: Subtract 7	
18	11
12	**5**
17	**10**
19	**12**

Rule: Add 10	
5	15
9	**19**
12	**22**
14	**24**

Page 115

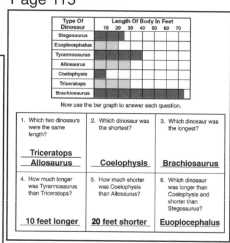

Type Of Dinosaur	Length Of Body In Feet						
	10	20	30	40	50	60	70
Stegosaurus							
Euoplocephalus							
Tyrannosaurus							
Allosaurus							
Coelophysis							
Triceratops							
Brachiosaurus							

Now use the bar graph to answer each question.

1. Which two dinosaurs were the same length? **Triceratops Allosaurus**	2. Which dinosaur was the shortest? **Coelophysis**	3. Which dinosaur was the longest? **Brachiosaurus**
4. How much longer was Tyrannosaurus than Triceratops? **10 feet longer**	5. How much shorter was Coelophysis than Allosaurus? **20 feet shorter**	6. Which dinosaur was longer than Coelophysis and shorter than Stegosaurus? **Euoplocephalus**